McGRAW-HILL STUDIES IN POLITICAL SCIENCE
FRITZ MORSTEIN MARX, Editor

THE POLITICS OF MODERN SPAIN

THE POLITICS

OF

MODERN SPAIN

BY

FRANK E. MANUEL

FOREWORD BY

FRITZ MORSTEIN MARX

FIRST EDITION

McGRAW-HILL BOOK COMPANY, Inc.

NEW YORK AND LONDON

1938

THE MAPLE PRESS COMPANY, YORK, PA.

To

THE WOMAN WHO SPAN

FOREWORD

Until the outbreak of the present Civil War Spain was known primarily for her past. To most contemporaries hers was the museum appeal. The picture of her political realities remained dim. Since then a flood of "interpretations" of the Spanish tragedy has added confusion to dimness. Few of the current "interpretations" aspire to meet the acute need for an appraisal both based on facts and looking beyond facts. This book does.

When its author took leave of his academic work in order to help develop the educational program of the American labor movement, he had already established himself in the minds of his students as an authority on the history of the French working class. Before his extensive research on this topic was brought to a close, Dr. Manuel responded to the opportunity offered him to survey the political scene in turbulent Spain. His findings—placed in broad historical perspective—are here presented.

But to point to the author's command of the relevant data would alone not suffice to suggest the character of his analysis. A piece of brilliant writing, it is at the same time compact and swiftly moving. A political study in the best sense, it combines the features of social, economic, and cultural inquiry in a forceful synthesis. A document pregnant with personal conviction, it testifies no less strongly to the spirit of scholarship. Though impatient with ecclesiastical shortcomings, Dr. Manuel is not without a faith. Generous in his invective for the intellectuals, he yet invokes the freedom of intellect. Despite his exorcism of fascist ideology, he does not hesitate to turn the spotlight on the deficiencies of leftist Spanish leaders.

To the student of revolutionary movements and revolutionary technique, Spain, rather than Russia, is becoming the standard laboratory. Dr. Manuel's book makes this laboratory widely available. The formulae evolved by fate and human cunning in a long series of coups and countercoups are now being put to a final test in the People's Front experiment on the one hand and in Franco's one-party venture on the other. *El Caudillo's* new

National Party—on whose Grand Council no less than three women have found seats—is thus far an organization only in the formal sense. The traditionalist elements in its membership still respect the insignia of bygone days, while most of the Falangist militiamen have become more pronounced in their espousal of the fascist brand of a peasant-minded "social revolution." To what extent the Catholic Church will be able to cope with the novel slogans of a Spanish Phalanx under German-Italian tutelage remains to be seen. Nor have all cleavages been bridged over in the loyalist camp.

Whatever the outcome of the Civil War, three facts seem indisputable. First, as the disastrous conflict drags on, each day will intensify the division of the nation against itself and make the task of reconstruction more formidable. Second, reconciliation cannot be inaugurated by the sword. Thus the ultimate disintegration of one or the other army of liberty is bound to beget a reign of terror and vengeance hailed by the victorious side as an indispensable purgatory. And third, a "reborn" Spain will be a serious potential threat to the *status quo* in the Old World. She might well share the destiny of other late arrivals by *nolens volens* becoming a major European headache.

FRITZ MORSTEIN MARX.

ADAMS HOUSE,
   HARVARD UNIVERSITY.

ACKNOWLEDGMENTS

Thanks are due to the author's friends, Dr. Norton E. Long and Mr. Edwin Mims, Jr., for a careful reading of the proofs; to Professors Edith Fishtine and Miguel Antonio Peña and Mr. José K. P. de Varon for helpful suggestions on specific points; and to Mr. Carl B. Shapiro for preparing the index.

The author is indebted to Houghton Mifflin Company for permission to quote from *Counter-Attack in Spain*, by Ramón Sender; to Foreign Policy Association, Inc., for permission to quote from *Spain under the Dictatorship*, by Agnes S. Waddell; to The University of Chicago Press for permission to quote from *Toward the New Spain*, by Joseph A. Brandt; to *Foreign Affairs* for permission to quote from "The October Revolution in Spain," by Luis Araquistáin; to Faber and Faber, Ltd., for permission to quote from *Seven Red Sundays*, by Ramón Sender; to Cassell and Company, Ltd., for permission to quote from *The Truth about Spain*, by G. H. B. Ward; to *The Irish Monthly*, Dublin, for permission to quote from "Gil Robles and Spanish Politics," by P. McBride.

The *Nation*, *The New York Times*, and the *Christian Science Monitor* have kindly assented to the use of materials which appeared in articles written by the author.

F. E. M.

Boston, Mass.,
January, 1938.

CONTENTS

CONTENTS

Chapter I

THE UGLINESS OF DECAY

Though El Greco, Ribera, and Velázquez, Cervantes, Lope de Vega, and Calderón mounted to the apex of human creation in the arts, Spain in the seventeenth century experienced only faint reverberations of the scientific enthusiasm which agitated the north of Europe. Spanish marriages provided *casus belli* for the continent, even as they would for the next 300 years; intellectual converse was rare. Science, religious toleration, and manufacturing supported one another in England and the Netherlands. Spain revered the other Trinity, which was glorified with *autos da fé*, spectacles devotional and entertaining, well into the eighteenth century. A few Spanish thinkers did question the wisdom of their country's absolute estrangement from the movement of scientific ideas in Western Europe, and even cautiously suggested that Spanish orthodox tradition might allow itself to be colored with the debonair manner and wit of French culture. But the innovators were overwhelmed by the abuse of devout Spaniards. Spain must remain true to her ancient faith and avoid the corruption of the foreigners across the Pyrenees.

When in 1700 the Frenchman Philip V, grandson of Louis XIV, came to occupy the throne vacated by the Spanish Hapsburgs, he found a shrunken empire and a people drained by the terrible wars of the past 200 years. Gold and silver from Peru and Mexico had blinded the Spaniards to their own industrial potentialities.[1] The precious metals had not long remained in Spanish coffers, but had found their way into the north of Europe, where they stimulated productive activities in France, England, and the Dutch provinces. Under the new Bourbon dynasty Spain remained stagnant; there were peace and poverty. The church, with its tentacles penetrating all strata of society, was the dominant force. It owned outright a fourth of the cultivated lands in the kingdom, and its revenues were augmented by

1

sundry dues on the other three-fourths. Even though the head
of the state was a layman, Spain appeared to be more a theocracy
than a monarchy. With few mitigating circumstances, the
ecclesiastical hegemony was the dominion of pure ignorance.

The autobiography of the honest scholar Diego de Torres y
Villarroel bears witness to the disintegration of university life
under the aegis of the church.[2] In one passage he describes a
competition in 1726 for the chair of mathematics and astrology
at the ancient University of Salamanca, in which he was adjudged
the victor by the riotous cries and applause of an assembled
multitude of students and peasants. The new science was
prohibited in Spain, while theology had been allowed to decay.
Learning divine and secular was abandoned by an indolent
clergy, who sank ever deeper into idolatrous practices. The
grandeur of medieval churches was desecrated by the introduction
of dressed dolls. Religious organizations expended their
wealth upon the pomp of semibarbaric and gaudy ceremonies.
Of the people it was said: "They die of hunger beside Madonnas
bedecked with diamonds."[3]

Meliorists in a Theocracy

The only potential rival to the clergy in the eighteenth century
was the Bourbon king, who became the spearhead of an attack
against the theocracy. He attempted to reassert his absolute
power by expelling the Jesuits (1767), humbling the Inquisition
until it was a mere tool of the monarchy, and wresting from
Rome a concordat which placed the most important offices of
the ecclesiastical hierarchy in the hands of the secular authority. By the end of the century the royal administrative sallies
against the church were advancing with great vigor, when a gust
of irreligious liberalism from across the Pyrenees suddenly revived
the slumbering clergy. Stories of French Jacobin atrocities
roused the people to a defense of their ancient religion and its
fanatical priests, and once again the spirit of bigotry settled "like
a foul mist on the goodly promise of the land."[4]

In the midst of a general stultification, moved by the misery
of the peasants and the decline of the monarchy, a few stray
meliorists—Jovellanos, Aranda, Campomanes, Pérez y López,
and Florida-Blanca, men who had read the French *philosophes*
and economists—marshalled their projects of reform.[5] In 1785

Pérez y López wrote the *Principles of the true order of nature,*[6] which demanded aid for the poor and attacked the preservation of vast uncultivated *latifundios,* those great domains awarded to the military and religious orders after the expulsion of the Moors. Learned journals printed anonymous plans for the economic revival of Spain. The *Semanario Erudito* for 1790 published a curious pamphlet entitled *Cause for the decadence of the Spanish monarchy and its effective cure.* In opposition to prevailing notions of Spanish incompetence the writer, with characteristic pride, maintained that the ingenuity of Spaniards, when they applied themselves to arts and sciences, was equal if not superior to that of foreigners. And yet he had to admit that Spain swarmed with thousands of paupers, who often maimed themselves in order to pursue their fruitless occupation. In this reformist's opinion, tinged with a bit of eighteenth century materialism, government stimulus alone might force the people to engage in productive labor.

What if all the magnificent objects which surround Majesty in Spain, goods for the royal household, guards, and army, were manufactured at home, instead of being imported from northern Europe? Since there are no factories in Spain, why not build them? Their utility can easily be demonstrated by a comparison of the welfare of those villages where some traditional industry, however insignificant, has been preserved, with the poverty of those which languish without any such support. To wealthy merchant-manufacturers who desired assurance of a market the homely Spanish economist appealed in the name of both interest and God. Investments at home would be more secure than the overseas enterprises on which Spaniards had concentrated their energies ever since the conquest of the Americas. And in aiding the poor by providing work, the rich men would obtain the blessing of God. What madness to submit to other risks and to refuse "to contract with God, who is most faithful in his promises of eternal felicity . . . !"[7] Other reformers, with equal fervor, subscribed to this curious intermingling of religious argument and economic reasoning in an effort to bring about an industrial renascence. They descanted on the lands which lay fallow, on the rivers which could be rendered navigable, on the evils of contemporary judicial organization, and on the depopulation of the countryside. After traveling through France, Germany, and England, one writer was still sanguine about the economic prospects of his native land. "It can be explained after the manner of the scholastics: there is neither very much industry nor great fertility in Spain: *in actu, concedo, in potentia, nego.*"[8]

Practical possibilities of reform were, however, meager, for the Bourbon kings proved themselves no hardier in their administration than the last Hapsburgs. The libertinism of noble society in late eighteenth century Spain could vie with any European aristocracy. The court was a more sullen and perverted Versailles; Charles IV was a weakling; Godoy, his prime minister, was a usurping major-domo.[9] Goya's famous portrait of the royal family leaves nothing but superficialities to a mere verbal description.

Napoleon "the Jacobin"

Napoleon, sensing the weakness of the Bourbon, ordered him into his presence at Bayonne (1808), where, out of terror or stupidity, the King of Spain delivered up the throne like a petty vassal. But his subjects refused to accept the new foreigner. The Spanish War of Independence against the French invaders revealed that centuries of isolation had knit the people together in spite of the oppression of the nobility and the darkness of the church. Napoleon came bearing gifts of liberty and was spurned; the proud Spaniards disdainfully nicknamed his emissary Joseph "Joe Bottles." Though the ruling classes of Spain had abandoned their land to Napoleon, there was a *levée en masse* which in long years of guerilla warfare sapped the strength of the Emperor. French battalions which captured city after city, and even occupied Madrid, could not force the Spaniards to lay down their arms. No foreigner would be endured who brought them toleration and liberalism in a Jacobin emperor's cloak. "Say, Napoleon," cried a pamphleteer, "what did our beloved kings do to you that you betrayed them in a manner terrible enough to be written in the annals of Spain with letters of blood?"[10] The horrors of this War of Independence have been universalized by Goya in *Los desastres de la guerra*. The heroism of the men and women who fought in defense of their country engraved lasting images on the consciousness of the Spaniards. In the fall of 1936 memories of the two sieges of Saragossa, 1808–1809, were revived to bolster the courage of the Loyalist militia in Madrid.

Amid the havoc of the Napoleonic Wars a group of liberal intellectuals, patriotic army officers, and middle-class city dwellers met in a Cortes at Cadiz to revive the medieval tradition of Spanish "liberties," which had long since fallen into decay. Naturally, their Constitution of 1812 was profoundly influenced by contemporary English and French doctrines, and though the document which they promulgated preserved Catholicism as the state religion, there were enough references to humanity, national sovereignty, and liberty to terrify and outrage the clergy, who set upon these "philosophical insects" with their lampoons. "Humanity," wrote one clerical pamphleteer, "means love for evil-doers, piety with prostitutes, inflexible harshness towards churchmen and monks, and a total neglect of God."[11] The patriotic officers and city people, advancing as torchbearers of enlightenment, were confronted by the blunt obscurantism of a church which maintained: "If philosophy must lead us to lose faith and religion, then let us better remain ignorant and uncultured."[12]

During the seven years of the War of Independence the survival of the nation had been identified with the old religious order, and the heir to the throne, the imbecile Ferdinand, became the symbol of national regeneration. Hence when Napoleon "the Jacobin" was finally defeated, the *camarilla* which gathered about the King were able to take violent reprisals from all liberal factions tainted with foreign ideas. Even if Ferdinand VII was a changeling who broke his oath and annulled the Constitution of 1812, accepted it again in 1820 in the presence of menacing army detachments, and reannulled it in 1823 when the French Royalists sent an expedition of 100,000 men to his aid, the mass of the people, in solemn protest against the revolutionary Gallicizers, welcomed back the clerical scourge and the Society of the Exterminating Angel to purge them of their sins.

Though Rafael del Riego's revolt in 1820, the movement of a small army band under masonic influence, was a fiasco, it left behind a libertarian image. His moving column had sung the Hymn of Riego, and the anthem echoed through the century. His execution provided the first great revolutionary martyr for modern Spain.[13]

Pronunciamientos and Fusillades

Soon after he had been secured on the throne by the Duke of Angoulême, Ferdinand VII was molested by ultraroyalist Catholic protagonists in his own ranks, who, under the rubric of the Apostolicals, grouped themselves about the Infante Don Carlos. When Ferdinand, a wan object of deathbed intrigues, left the throne to the Queen Regent María Cristina and her daughter Isabella by a revival of Charles IV's Pragmatic Sanction of 1789, these fanatical zealots, the Carlists, denounced it as a violation of the Salic law, which excluded females from the throne. In 1833 the Queen Regent, confronted by 200,000 hostile Carlist soldiers, with the backing of the Central Powers for the Pretender, had to rely upon the constitutional monarchies of France and England for the preservation of her daughter's throne. She was even forced to beg support from the Spanish liberals, who forthwith took advantage of her predicament to demand constitutional reform. When the liberals themselves divided into the less ardent, the Moderates under Martínez de la Rosa, and those who sought severe measures against the clergy, the Progressists, a tricornered struggle was initiated.

Mendizábal, a Jew by extraction, financier and Progressist, became prime minister and inaugurated a scheme whereby extensive measures of secularization would force the church itself to pay for the war against the Carlist fanatics. The inevitable reaction in favor of the Moderates followed, which in turn brought forth the restoration of their alternates, the Progressists. This time, in 1837, the Progressists were sufficiently emboldened to draft a constitution. Yet no sooner had Spain begun to enjoy the fruits of revived liberalism when a Carlist rebellion, which lasted for more than two years, overshadowed projects of reform. The Queen Regent María Cristina owed her daughter's throne to the military genius of General Espartero, who in 1839 finally forced the Carlist chief to accept peace and a kiss at Vergara. Then, in harmony with the prevailing political temper, the victorious commander, a leader of the Progressists, became Duque de la Victoria, drove out María Cristina, who had discredited herself by her sexual follies, and assumed the regency himself

When the Moderates returned to power in 1848 they initiated a period of comparative peace and administrative reorganization which lasted until 1854, a rare epoch in nineteenth century Spain. Two generals, Narváez and O'Donnell, protected the young Queen Isabella and guided her through the diplomatic trials of a Spanish royal marriage by presenting her with a perverted cousin for a husband. Spain had become a prey to the rival interests of England and France, her erstwhile protectors, and before the prince consort was chosen, the two patrons, forgetful of their solid virtues, engaged in an eighteenth century cabal. Queen Victoria backed the Progressists; Louis Philippe supported the Moderates. In 1854 the Progressists reappeared under General Espartero. There ensued fourteen years of petty squabbling during which the Moderate generals, Narváez and O'Donnell, issued military *pronunciamientos* whenever their rivals were in power, and the new Progressist leader, General Prim y Prats, reciprocated in kind. "The same dogs with other collars," it was said.

The revolutions, *pronunciamientos*, conspiracies, fusillades, church burnings, and constitutions hardly outliving the day of their proclamation, which checkered the turbulent period from 1808 to 1868, were the ill-defined expressions of an ill-defined desire on the part of the third estate to attain to some measure of consideration in the government.[14] In this effort liberal army officers and bankers mingled with workers and shopkeepers. Middle-class revolutions which succeeded each other in France, Italy, and Germany were a continually renewed object lesson, for the traditional isolation of Spain should not, by the nineteenth century, be exaggerated. Normally, the Spanish middle class would have preferred a constitutional monarchy to a republic, which might thrust the social problem into the arena and lead to such disastrous consequences as the June Days of Paris, 1848. But the weak Spanish bourgeoisie could not organize political demonstrations in its own right comparable to those of the French bankers and industrialists of 1830. It did not know its course, and the harrowing incidents of these sixty years are the chronicle of its temporary alliances, lunges forward, and frightened retreats. Vacillation debilitated the half-hearted attempts of the bourgeoisie, and the most it could achieve was a more liberal *camarilla* or a less clerical despotism.

The Revolution of 1868

During the last years of her reign Queen Isabella II had been dependent upon the armed forces of Narváez and O'Donnell, who quelled Carlist uprisings on the extreme right and suppressed

Republican propagandists on the left. When these generals died, in 1867 and 1868 respectively, she was left alone, a pawn in the intrigues of the two parties which for more than thirty years had alternated in the ministries, the Moderates and the Progressists, those peculiar Spanish euphemisms for more and less corrupt politicians. When the Progressists, representing primarily the upper middle class, became seriously troubled by the growing subservience of the Queen to the clerical elements, they resolved to oust the Bourbons. Under Generals Serrano and Prim y Prats they dexterously engineered a revolution. Exiled General Prim landed at Cadiz and proclaimed the sovereignty of the nation in the same city where the Cortes of 1812 had sat. The Queen, vacationing in the Basque provinces, had no loyal forces and preferred to cross the border into France rather than to resist. This was the Revolution of 1868, the final attempt of the bourgeoisie to strike out against the enemy, a well-concerted rebellion after sixty years of tergiversation. At last the discontented elements had formed a united third estate, after the pattern rendered classical by the French Revolution—the cooperation of the upper middle class and the lower, propped by the promised support of the workers.

General Prim's early pronouncements had a style pregnant with momentous change, "To arms, citizens, to arms! . . . [A] sole banner, the regeneration of the country," and even a middling good definition of revolt, "To destroy in the midst of tumult the obstacles which systematically oppose the welfare of nations is the mission of armed revolution."[15] But once the play began, the standard divisions within the third estate revealed themselves. The *haute bourgeoisie* broke away and rescinded its revolutionary proclamations. The Jacobins (in Spain the Democrats) did not want a king, even a constitutional one. In spite of opposition, a monarchy remained the ideal of the Progressists, and for many months the world was entertained by the spectacle of a Cortes begging every dynasty in Europe for a princelet to rule the Spanish people. In foreign courts there was no enthusiasm for a throne which military men, invading the palace every few years, filled or vacated as they chose. When General Prim, the star of the Girondists, finally imported Amadeo of Savoy, the king maker was assassinated and the youthful King, surnamed Macaroni I, was a lost soul

amid the turmoil of a strange class conflict in a country whose
national idiosyncrasies he could not fathom. The bewilderment
of these years was intensified by the reappearance of the Carlists,
so that the Cortes was divided into countless overlapping groups
which formed fantastic coalitions on any given issue. At one
point the papal nuncio in attacking the election of forlorn
Amadeo joined the radicals, who shouted: "Death to God!"

The oratorical small bourgeoisie, attended by their lawyers
and inspired by professors filled with blasts of idealist philosophy
from Karl Krause, an early nineteenth century German thinker,
were finally indulged the adventure of a republican regime.
After Amadeo abdicated in 1872, the intellectuals were summoned
in February, 1873, to establish that system of harmony which
their mediocre German philosopher, popularized in Spain by
Sanz del Río, had preached as the ideal order of society—law,
liberty, justice, truth, and beauty. Freedom of religious worship
for all creeds, the initial step, had already been won by the
flourishes of the Republican Castelar, the noblest orator in Spain.
His speech on religious toleration, delivered on April 12, 1869,
has been hailed as one of the most extraordinary manifestations
of the century, even though the printed words may now appear
to be a stilted compendium of the excursions of his age into
sentimental liberalism. "Great is the religion of power," he
cried, "but greater far is the religion of love, great is the religion
of implacable justice, but even greater is the religion of merciful
forgiveness; and in the name of the Evangel, I come here to ask
that you write in your fundamental code religious freedom,
which is liberty, fraternity, equality among all men."[16]

Unfortunately, the small bourgeois intellectuals discovered
that the ears of the workers and the peasants were not attuned
to their delicate harmonies. The ethical ideal of *Krausismo*
interested the laborers of the soil far less than the possession of
land. When the workers did think in abstractions their ideals
were revolutionary and their slogans bore the imprint of Marx
and Bakunin. By 1870 Fanelli, a representative of the First
International Workingmen's Association, had already organized
a few workers' circles, though he was never quite certain himself
whether his revolutionary principles leaned more to the Socialism
of Marx or to the Anarchism of Bakunin. The pure middle-class
Democrats tried to appease their allies in the lower strata of

society with encomiums of the workingman and promises of social legislation; but the eloquent Castelar and his fellows could not countenance acts of violence perpetrated by workers without an orderly philosophy of life.

Ultimately, a breach with the amorphous groups of revolutionary workers reduced the Democrats to impotence. The Anarchists ventured a few heroic uprisings, like medieval *jacqueries;* the peasants burned fences which enclosed the village commons—now in the hands of a landlord, though only recently their own property on which they had been able to graze sheep or gather wood at will. Cities were seized by revolutionary councils, which declared them free and independent communes; the red flag was hoisted at Cartagena—a Turkish emblem was the only one available. In the midst of the confusion, ideologists of the middle class were giving violent utterance in the Cortes to divergent conceptions of a republic. Should it be unitary or federal, or what combination of separatism, local autonomy, federalism, and centralization should be the official Spanish formula? Confronted by long-winded debates about the nature of executive and administrative power, the anarchist began to feel even more strongly the validity of his a-political doctrines. He became as relentless an enemy of this regime of bourgeois political theorists as he had been of the feudal monarchy. In clashes with republican troops the revolutionary workers were crushed. Middle-class intellectuals with blood on their hands lost confidence in their own power of organization and action.

The restorationist feudal elements thus had an opportunity to re-form their ranks and to call upon a general, Pavía this time, who was entrusted with the task of effecting a *coup d'état*, the traditional solution. He swept out the debaters, killed the rioters, and in 1874 summoned Isabella's son, Alfonso XII, to the throne. The night cry of village watchmen—*Viva la República Democrática Federal!*—was superseded by *Ave Maria Purissima.* The *intransigentes*, uncompromising revolutionaries, hotly pursued by the army, took to the hills, where they lived like animals on the roots they gathered. Sometimes they descended upon a village, sacked it, then returned to their lair.[17] Local officials had stringent orders for dealing with any disaffection. "Do not telegraph a rising unless you can, at the same time, telegraph that you have shot half the rioters."

The Rule of the Caciques

After successfully mopping up stray revolutionary centers, the restored Bourbons, in 1876, presented the people with a constitution. Peace reigned for a quarter of a century, and the absolute rule of local overlords was established upon a firm foundation—the rule of the *caciques*. *Cacique* was the Indian name for tribal chieftain, which soon after the conquests in America passed into Spanish as the epithet for a local notable. By the nineteenth century it was used to designate a politician with a following in a commune or province, who exercised broad political powers without holding any legal office commensurate with his influence. Azcárate, a nineteenth century political theorist, author of a pungent analysis of *caciquismo*, considered it a modern adaptation of feudalism. During the troubles of the first 70 years of the nineteenth century, strong men rose to be both protectors and masters of little communes, whole districts, and even extensive provinces. Since most governmental changes, though effected by *coup d'état*, had to assume a semblance of constitutional form, the ministers in Madrid needed local politicians to organize the elections. The ministers were thus dependent upon the provincial *caciques*, who in turn recognized their superiors in this oligarchy as the first of the *caciques*.

After the Restoration of 1874 the stabilizing influence of ministerial cycles abolished the need for violent *pronunciamientos*, as the two newly formed major parties, the Conservatives under Cánovas and the Liberals under Sagasta, had amicably agreed upon a system of regular rotation in office. During this peaceful period the *caciques* grew even more powerful than they had been before 1868. They entrenched themselves as absolute rulers in their localities, key men upon whom all judicial and administrative agencies were frankly dependent. Their allegiance was due only to the higher *cacique* whom they served well in return for an assurance of exclusive domination in their own areas. Joaquín Costa's pointed *Oligarchy and caciquismo as the actual form of government in Spain* (1901) has laid bare the fissures which this system cut through the body politic:

Each region, each province found itself under the overlordship of an irresponsible individual, who may or may not have been a deputy, without whose consent not a single piece of paper was moved, not an affair settled, not a decision rendered, not a judge appointed, not a functionary chosen, not a public work undertaken. For him the laws did not exist. In order to know the outcome of a trial . . . you did not ask yourself whether you had right or the laws on your side; it was necessary to know whether the *cacique* had some interest in the case, whether he would stay neutral, whether he would be for you or against you. . . . Taxes were not levied in accordance with official regulations, but rather in accordance with the will of the *cacique*, the interests of his clique, the pressure which it was proper to exert upon neutrals, the punishment fitting for them. He who did not submit paid double. . . . Appeals were stopped or they lay in the dossiers. Roads were not constructed after the design of engineers, but in accordance with the situation of the *cacique's* property or of the villages which were subject to him. . . . In exchange he gave his creatures *carte blanche* and protection, allowing them to do what they liked with the monies of the communes and the rights of fellow-citizens. The *cacique's* fief was delimited by the supreme chiefs; sometimes it comprised a region, sometimes a province, sometimes one or two districts; and in turn it was divided into sub-fiefs. . . . The whole formed a closely-knit system which held the country prisoner."[18]

When crops were bad the *cacique* lent the peasants money and extorted so monstrous a rate of interest that sometimes all the peasants of a village were indebted to him. Through his control of irrigation he could at will provide their fields with water or allow them to become parched and sterile. When he forced the peasants to the wall during years of drought, they sold the common pasture lands which had been their patrimony for ages; the enclosure movement was still in progress when the Republic of 1931 came into being. In conjunction with the village priest, the *cacique* held the peasant body and soul.

The Cortes, which met in accordance with the provisions of the Constitution of 1876, was not divided by opposing economic interests, a class stratification, or abstract ideals. It was an arena for petty maneuvers and intrigues, for here were allotted concessions from the central favor-disbursing agencies. The booty which *caciques* divided among one another comprised posts in the army, the church, and the administrative bureaucracy, and as the demand for these sinecures grew acute, Spain became burdened with a load of officials who drew salaries without fulfilling any useful function in the state. To the village peasant the whole governmental mechanism in Madrid was an incomprehensible maze. The peasant rarely moved from the district where he was born; local customs were preserved and the distinct dialects of various provinces survived; to these he owed his loyalties. Spanish patriotism was a favorite topic with the phrasemongers in Madrid; actually, the country was unified only in a formal administrative sense. Emissaries of the same government penetrated into the tiniest villages, isolated in the mountains, to collect taxes—the most significant contact of the peasant with the state. The services which are associated with the modern commonwealth were never provided.

During the Restoration and the Regency for the young Alfonso XIII (1874–1902), deputies of both the party in power and the official opposition were named in the antechambers of the minister of the interior. The Pact of Prado between the rival leaders, Cánovas and Sagasta, had assured due respect for both factions, so that one clique, when temporarily in eclipse, indulged only in the most discreet censure of its partner. Local *caciques* of the two parties had understandings with each other which paralleled the arrangements of the ministers in the capital. Political chieftains in Madrid were often of noble lineage, but those at the bottom of the scale, the *tiranos chicos*, burdened with the task of swinging elections, came to their posts with criminal records.[19] Sagasta's election law reform of 1890, which granted suffrage to all male citizens, failed to undermine the power of the *caciques*. No matter what modifications were introduced the *caciques* publicly boasted that they had techniques at their disposal to circumvent the new impediments to their rule. The most elementary proposals of reformers were doomed to failure in their initial stages, and those rare projects which did make their way through the Cortes were rendered meaningless by the real executive power embodied in the *caciques*. After 1900 protests against the corroded system of local administration piled up. Even conservative ministers, orating on the sorry state of the nation, voiced severe criticism of that very monopoly of political influence upon which their existence in office was founded. In 1907 Prime Minister Maura delivered himself of an eloquent denunciation of *caciquismo* and then proceeded to "make" a general election in which the *caciques* had freer play than ever before.

It was inevitable that so elaborate a system of corruption should breed universal disdain for existing party politics. Spaniards remained proud, boastful, and foolhardy in their international relations, prepared for war at the slightest provocation, even against overwhelming odds. At home they heaped scorn upon anyone who engaged in politics and considered the very act of participation a stigma. That insignificant minority which sought change had recourse to the anarchist movement if they were violent, the socialist if they were mild. Professors of law published reports diagnosing the disease of *caciquismo*, tracing its history, prescribing simple remedies; but the mass of the people could see no salvation in a barrage of words. When elections unfavorable to a *cacique* were annulled by the mere statement that the tabulation had been faulty, the average Spaniard refused to go to the polls.

The Spiritual Halo

Paradoxically enough, this political gangrene did not preclude the enrollment of many progressive acts of legislation on the statute books. At the turn of the century, deputies of the Cortes seem to have amused themselves by copying, sometimes verbatim, the most advanced laws of the constitutional regimes of Western Europe. These laws, duly signed by the executive power, were a baroque façade for venality of office and administrative ineptitude. Laws remained hidden away in official bulletins; no one heeded them. As Joaquín Costa, in pessimist mood, phrased it: "Things have not changed because liberty has become paper and not flesh." The legal forms of feudalism had for the most part been eradicated. The Inquisition, feudal privileges, tithes, and *corvées* had been slowly abolished after each one of the *coups d'état* of the nineteenth century. The Rights of Man, a codification of civil and criminal law, and popular suffrage had been introduced. But the facts remained the same—feudalism in decay. A hodgepodge of theoretically progressive legislation and reactionary practice produced a system of administrative government which was arbitrary—not absolute. This arbitrariness of local officials was more akin to anarchy than to either royal absolutism or constitutional monarchy.[20]

So decadent a political system, nourished by the toil of ill-fed peasants and half-starved city workers, was obviously in dire need of a spiritual halo. The most fanatical Catholic party, the Carlists, defeated in the Civil Wars, was a declining force, though the absolutism of its pronouncements still excited the fervor of ignorant peasants in Navarra and in the Basque provinces. As late as 1910, Don Juan de Clazabel, leader of the Basque Integralists, propounded this extraordinary medieval doctrine: "We desire to render unto God the things that are God's, and unto Caesar the things that are Caesar's, but we wish Caesar to humiliate himself before God, and Church and State to exist united, with the temporal body submitted to the spiritual power, even as the carnal body is subdued by the soul."[21] When it became evident, however, that this Carlist ideal was beyond attainment and therefore impolitic to espouse, the church, reluctantly enough, accepted a position which was less presumptuous, though by no means inferior in its ultimate influence. The Bourbon king and the church abandoned their medieval controversy about the relative powers of the spiritual and the temporal spheres and united in preserving Spain from those evils of modernism which threatened to drown them in a common tub.

Under the pseudoconstitutional regime the church, posing as a purely spiritual influence, was provided with more varied opportunities for the accumulation of wealth than any jealous sixteenth century autocrat would have allowed. The riches of the institution soon became proverbial; its anonymity always prevented them from becoming statistical. It may be the exaggeration of an anticlerical that the numerous religious orders controlled more than a third of the wealth of the country. Certainly the foresight of the church in engaging in every conceivable form of industrial activity and commercial transaction, in contrast with the nobility which still considered participation in economic production a disparagement, gathered a bountiful harvest. Before the Bourbon Restoration rival generals and politicians, whenever they came into office, mulcted the church with such regularity that its capacity for financial recuperation must arouse wonderment.

In 1826 one ecclesiastic was provided for every 91 inhabitants; through the vicissitudes of the century this number was reduced, but with the persecution of religious orders in early twentieth century France, the influx of fresh monks and nuns foretold a rapid increase.   The Concordat of 1851 had vaguely limited the number of religious orders in Spain; the Law of Associations of 1887 had submitted most of them to the statutes which governed ordinary organizations.   In practice, the economic fruits of ecclesiastical industry, carefully distributed in emoluments to civil officials, always preserved the church outside the pale of the law.   The income from plenary indulgences was enough to keep thousands of inmates in convents and monasteries well-fed and to maintain bishops in awe-inspiring luxury.   By contrast, the lot of uninfluential curates in hundreds of tiny hamlets was as wretched as that of their parishioners.

Unless the religious tenets were wholeheartedly accepted, the tactics of the Spanish church hierarchy were likely to arouse a vigorous anticlericalism.   The horrors which were sometimes perpetrated by rapacious priests to secure the inheritance of the faithful for the mother church led to scandals which smelled of the dregs of human existence.   The rights of civil marriage and of decent burial without the benediction of the church were wrested from the clergy in the early years of the twentieth century only after violent struggles, marked by disgusting incidents during which the bodies of the dead were desecrated.   In other countries of Western Europe Catholicism was constrained to make compromises with a new social order; but the papal encyclicals which featured concepts of social justice in order to maintain the hold of Catholicism over the masses brought less change in the temper of the Spanish churchmen than elsewhere on the Continent.   French Catholicism was humiliated and forced to submit to the reforms of Premier Combes; in Spain the clerics grew more arrogant.

Loyola and St. John of the Cross were succeeded by crude charlatans who displayed their stigmata to a credulous multitude; proud apologists of the church were replaced by obsequious servants who dawdled about in the antechambers of the monarch. In a country where utilitarian instincts were not well-developed the Jesuits alone learned to keep accounts with meticulous care.   The coffers of ancient cathedrals were filled with gold, the contribution of 20,000,000 ignorant peasants who dragged out their miserable existence in this world and quaked in terror of what might overcome them in the next.   The Vatican reaped its share from the continued devotion of the faithful in its last stronghold on the continent and in return munificently dropped red caps on the heads of its successful Spanish clergymen. Even when the church had ceased to possess the souls of the urban middle classes it still could enforce overt religious observance and collect its monies. Monks and nuns in other countries performed social functions; when Spanish women entered religious establishments they were entombed forever within the convent walls. Religion had never been particularly spiritualized in Spain and a good measure of idolatry and primitive earthiness survived in most ceremonies. The church fostered superstition and multiplied the number of miracle-performing images of the Virgin. During Holy Week in Seville the flagellants in the processions lashed themselves until they won the applause of gracious ladies upon whose clothes they spurted blood.[22] Small wonder that there were secret groups in Spain who shouted: "Crush the infamous one!"

Proletarian Martyrs

Ever since the fiasco of the First Republic, the land-owning "feudals" and the clergy had enjoyed the monetary support of a remorseful group of financiers and the tacit consent of the middle classes. Revolutionary workers, who alone refused to accept the resurrection of the old regime, became outlaws. They conspired in secret meeting places, beyond the confines of organized society. Their unions were dissolved, their leaders were tortured, their means of propaganda were destroyed. In spite of this oppression they continued to exist, an underground movement growing in strength with the gradual progress of industrialization in Spain. Fortified by the blood of their martyrs, hatred for all things connected with feudal or bourgeois society smoldered in their hearts. Sporadic outbursts of the anarchists were followed by bitter reprisals, but the Civil Guards, a corps of military police founded by General Narváez, could not wipe the revolutionaries off the face of the earth. In frantic attempts to destroy them, the government of the Spanish Bourbons, like the Romanovs at the other end of the Continent, resorted to the provocation of terrorist outbreaks.

Officials themselves planted bombs, that they might with more apparent justification launch fierce onslaughts against suspected workers. In the Barcelona uprising of 1909 heroes were born;

they died in the torture chambers of Montjuic. Isolated from middle-class agitation, the workers' movement in Spain had an almost independent existence. The proletariat was not buttressed by revolutionary leaders and thinkers from the upper strata, which though casting into the ranks of the workers opportunists, weaklings, and traitors has also provided them with solid theoreticians and strategists. When Francisco Ferrer, a rare exception, came to the working classes of Catalonia with new educational plans, he was hastily put out of the way in Barcelona (1909) by one of those judicial murders which make a travesty of legal institutions.[23]

Whenever the pent-up rage of workers and peasants would flare forth in church burnings and assassinations, the spectacle of these furious men appalled the middle classes and bound them with ever firmer ties to the existing regime. The bourgeois who might otherwise have relished a taste of Voltairianism was terrified by the revolutionaries and was prepared to bear the burden of the church, the nobility, and the king with trepidation and with gratitude.

"The Generation of '98"

Only one other group remained restive in late nineteenth century Spain, the intellectuals. Though in recent years they had acquired more learning and had multiplied their contacts with Western Europe, they remained humble in the face of the existing regime, for few of them would openly espouse the cause of the anarchist or the socialist agitators. Their uneasiness, nevertheless, increased as every new scientific discovery in Europe made the backwardness of their own country more striking. Defeat in the Spanish-American War finally confirmed their forebodings and emboldened them to reappear before the nation with a dramatic "Whither Spain?"

A group led by Francisco Giner de los Ríos had long since been struggling ahead with new educational institutions.[24] They were still deeply influenced by the philosophy of Karl Krause, and, after the victory of Prussian arms in 1871, they became even more profoundly impressed with the volume and depth of German scientific scholarship. Spain, they preached, would be saved through secular education. If politics had become corrupt and the universities had degenerated under Jesuit influence, then a small band of liberal intellectuals would teach in private schools outside the limits of official buildings. A select group of young men, inoculated with the moral virtues of *Krausismo*, trained in sports in imitation of the English colleges, and well-nurtured with factual knowledge, might raise a generation capable of reform.

The Free Institute of Education was founded to fulfill this mission, and many of its young students later became leaders of the Spanish Republic. In spite of Jesuit hostility the pioneers of secular education won a semiofficial status and in 1907, through great tact and diplomacy, they secured the establishment of a body with an extremely discreet title, *Junta para ampliación de estudios* (Committee for the Broadening of Studies), which provided young students with fellowships for education abroad. Knowledge gathered in foreign parts, it was hoped, would raise intellectual standards at home. It should be noted, however, that the education sponsored by this group, novel as it was for Spain, was destined primarily for middle-class elements, and its idealist character, its philosophy of law and justice, often blinded the young men of the Free Institute to the existence of brutal social conflicts. The lofty and rather academic idealism which the new teaching inspired would have been a fitting preparation for a more peaceful epoch than Spain was destined to know.

Intellectuals in another quarter, less obvious meliorists, brought forth reflections which were perhaps more brilliant, though far less useful socially than the doctrines of Francisco Giner. When Spain lost the last remnants of her great overseas empire during the Spanish-American War, many of her scholars took to writing keen essays on the nature of the Spanish people. In a sense, these pyschological studies of the "generation of '98" were a self-analysis which hoped to explain defeat and to justify the race before what was considered a decree of fate. The humiliation of the war, the victory of an upstart industrial nation over ancient Spain, stirred the intellectuals to prove to themselves and to the world that, though they did not excel in the techniques of a mechanized economy, they possessed other virtues in which no country could rival them. Their isolation during the past centuries, they expounded, had endowed them with a spirituality which no materialist Yankees could destroy. Though vanquished in war, their genius and its works would survive through the ages. The fruits of American civilization were meaningless to a Spaniard who had a soul, and contemplated life, death, and salvation.

Ángel Ganivet's *Idearium Español* (1897), the work of a prose Baudelaire, originated the *aperçus* about Spain's mission in European culture which were later popularized by Unamuno and Madariaga. His book, written a year before the disaster of Spain's defeat, diagnosed the illness of his country as *aboulia*,[25] loss of will power. Yet he was unwilling to prescribe any facile Europeanization as a remedy, for he believed that Spain would never regain her strength through servile imitation of alien processes and the adoption of strange manners. Ganivet called for a gathering of the waters in one place, a repatriation of Spanish energies within the boundaries of the land, an end to wasteful dispersion over the four corners of the earth.[26] Regeneration must come from within, he proclaimed with an Augustinian fervor which is all the more paradoxical since this extraordinary little book was completed in Helsingfors.

Fundamentally, the ideas of this group, which outlived Ganivet by many years and hardly changed a note in the theme for the next four decades, resolve themselves into a series of provocative antitheses. They contrast civilization with Spain's culture; intelligence with her intuition; sensuousness with her passion; rational scientificism with her arbitrary truths; technical achievement and physical comfort with her art and beauty; the leveling effects of democracy with her élite. Even if her peasants were ignorant and her city workers lived in squalor, even if she had one of the highest rates of illiteracy in Europe, poor means of communication, and bullfights which the French considered barbaric, Spain was the land with a soul. She had nurtured the genius of Cervantes and Goya, El Greco and Velázquez, Ignatius Loyola and St. John of the Cross. Her people understood death and therefore they knew life. Spain may have little knowledge in the Baconian sense, but she has wisdom.

Such notions trickled from the pen of Miguel de Unamuno and assumed the form of lively and pointed essays. The whole philosophy achieved its final expression in his masterpiece, the commentary on Don Quixote.[27] Europe's technical civilization is folly, he proclaimed. Europe is indulging in a debauch of optimism, while Spain preserves her noble pessimism. Spain may have had no rationalist mathematicians, but she has given birth to great mystics. No enterprising engineers transformed her landscape, but saints, and great sinners too, pulled at the vibrant strings of her soul. Whereas the rest of Europe has been involved in the dialectic of Roman right and wrong, the Spaniard has carved in relief the conflict between virtue and vice. The Spaniard is as fanatical as Loyola and as imaginative as Don Quixote. . . . Here were the ingredients, not yet combined, for a Spanish breed of intellectual fascism—*Edelfaschismus*.

The clergy, to be sure, were hostile to the slightest deviation of this group from true Catholic doctrine. In turn, when the intellectuals discovered to their dismay that the existing institutions of the church no longer harmonized with their ideal of spiritual exercises, they sometimes became anticlerical. Nevertheless they remained profoundly Catholic. They knew the meaning of vice and they were obsessed with sin.

In their day-to-day existence the intellectuals competed with each other for university chairs and wrote elegant articles in newspapers. They analyzed with subtlety the sleep which hung over them. They toyed with their decadence and pretended to revolt against it. Their whole outlook now seems akin to that of their Russian contemporaries who lived under similar social and economic conditions. Incapable of aping Europe, they denied it. Russia was Asia and mystic Greek orthodoxy. Spain was medieval Catholicism and the mysticism of the early Fathers. Europe was France—crass, logical, intelligent, superficial, scientific, without faith, glib, without understanding. To discover the sacred waters of regeneration Spain must fathom the mysteries of her own soul. . . . The literary philosophers thus made virtues out of their country's vicious heredity and extolled the material sufferings of their people as a prelude to spirituality. They invented a factitious national pyschology from the existing social fabric before them, and then proceeded to force it, like a strait-jacket, upon Spain of the middle ages and Spain of the future.

Spanish reformers less morose than the Unamuno type had a more mundane formula for their people. They soon comforted themselves that the defeat in war, humiliating though it may have been to Spanish pride, was not without positive advantage for the homeland. The mother country might finally cease to be a parasite living on the blood of colonial possessions whose inhabitants were exploited all the more ruthlessly because they were remnants of what had formerly been a great empire. Industrialists and capitalists would be constrained to turn their vital energies to the soil of Spain, delve into its fabulous resources, and revive productive forces in their native land. The overseas kingdoms would no longer be the focus of Spanish life.

Only a jolt was necessary to increase the tempo of modernization which had already made itself felt at the turn of the century. The impetus which set economic forces and new ideas into motion was given by that "mighty accelerator of events," the World War.

NOTES

1. See C. H. Haring, *Trade and Navigation between Spain and the Indies in the Time of the Hapsburgs*, Cambridge, 1918.
2. Diego de Torres y Villarroel (1696–1758), *Vida . . . escrita por el mismo*, new edition, pp. 115–117, Madrid, 1912.
3. See Georges Desdevises du Dezert, *L'Espagne de l'ancien régime. La société*, vol. I, Paris, 1897.
4. After William H. Prescott, *History of the Reign of Ferdinand and Isabella, the Catholic*, vol. III, pp. 491–492, Boston, 1838.
5. Gaspar Melchor de Jovellanos (1744–1811), the most noted of the group, was in 1912–1913 the subject of many learned memoirs in commemoration of the hundredth anniversary of his death. See Hilario Yaben Yaben, *Juicio crítico de las doctrinas de Jovellanos*, Madrid, 1913, and Gervasio de Artíñano y de Galdácano, *Jovellanos y su España*, Madrid, 1913. Jovellanos is famous in economic literature for his *Informe . . . en el expediente de ley agraria*, Madrid, 1795.
6. Antonio Javier Pérez y López (1736–1792), *Principios del orden esencial de la naturaleza*, Madrid, 1795.
7. "Causa de la decadencia de la Monarquía Española, y sus efectivos remedios," *Semanario Erudito*, vol. 29, p. 121, Madrid, 1790.
8. "Discursos políticos y económicos para que la España se restablezca de la situación en que se halla, é iguale en opulencia á las mayores monarquías de europa," *Semanario Erudito*, vol. 24, p. 47, Madrid, 1789.
9. See Hans Roger Madol, *Godoy, das Ende des alten Spanien. Der erste Diktator unserer Zeit*, Berlin, 1932.
10. "La voz de España á Napoleón," in Francisco Almarche Vázquez, *Ensayo de una bibliografía de folletos y papeles sobre la guerra de la independencia, publicados en Valencia 1808–1814*, p. 232, Saragossa, 1910.
11. *Diccionario Razonado. Manual para inteligencia de ciertos escritores que por equivocación han nacido en España. Aumentado con más de cincuenta voces, y una receta eficacísima para matar insectos filosóficos*, p. 40, Cadiz, 1811.
12. *Ibid.*, p. 2.
13. See Carmen de Burgos, *Don Rafael del Riego*, Madrid, 1931.

14. Only the novelist Pérez Galdós, one of the greatest although most neglected of the nineteenth century, has captured the intricacies of these movements in his *Episodios Nacionales.*

15. Edward Henry Strobel, *The Spanish Revolution,* p. 6, Boston, 1898.

16. Joseph A. Brandt, *Toward the New Spain,* p. 134, Chicago, 1933.

17. Hugh J. Rose, *Untrodden Spain and Her Black Country,* vol. I, pp. 35–36, London, 1875.

18. Joaquín Costa, *Oligarquía y caciquismo como la forma actual de gobierno en España,* pp. 8–10, Madrid, 1901.

19. *Ibid.,* p. 89.

20. See Henry Puget, *Le gouvernement local en Espagne,* vol. III, chap. 2, *La vie locale et la réalité derrière la loi,* pp. 189 ff., Paris, 1920.

21. G. H. B. Ward, *The Truth about Spain,* p. 47, London, 1911.

22. For fairly recent survivals of these practices see Mario Praz, *Unromantic Spain,* New York, 1929.

23. See William Archer, *The Life, Trial, and Death of Francisco Ferrer,* New York, 1911.

24. For a sympathetic account of Giner's group see John B. Trend, *The Origins of Modern Spain,* chaps. 4–7, Cambridge, 1934.

25. Ángel Ganivet (1862–1898), *Idearium Español,* p. 143, Granada, 1897.

26. *Ibid.,* p. 134.

27. Miguel de Unamuno y Jugo, *The Life of Don Quixote and Sancho according to Miguel de Cervantes Saavedra with comment by Miguel de Unamuno,* translated by Homer P. Earle, New York, 1927.

Chapter II

WARTIME PROSPERITY AND ITS AFTERMATH

In 1881 a German, von Conring, spent a few months in Morocco and returned with a book in which he called upon the Spaniards to extend their domain into Africa. He emphasized, however, that the conquest could never be achieved before Spain had been thoroughly revivified, and this would require the infusion of the purest blood in Europe into Spanish veins. The Madrid press was none too flattered by such proposals of alliance, proffered with Teutonic tact; on January 16, 1881, *El Imparcial* commented: "The basis of our future grandeur is certainly on the neighboring continent. But before dreaming of rescuing a people from slavery and barbarism, we should remain on our guard lest our fatherland be subjected to the despotism of a powerful ally. The northern coast of Africa might possibly be ours, but we ourselves, once the coast had been conquered, would become a camp for uhlans."[1]

In vain did England, France, and Germany, each in her own manner, coquet for an alliance with Spain. Privately, European statesmen deplored the instability of her government; liberals in particular despised her as a black hole of reaction; only poets of the picturesque could extol her virtues. And yet her strategic position forced consideration upon European diplomats. Spain had a long Mediterranean littoral, a promontory stretched out toward Africa, and an extended Atlantic coastline. She could become a satellite of one of the great powers, though certainly a rather troublesome one, for the notions of pride and the formulae of honor cultivated by Spanish *hidalgos* were not always comprehensible in other European chancelleries. Nations of Europe entering upon the era of imperialism, with its commercial interest and playful humanitarian superstructure, were confronted in Spain by drives-to-action from another age. The rather simple utilitarianism which in the late nineteenth century motivated most countries was still undeveloped in this peninsula.

What other powers considered naïve and childish maneuvers were in reality residues of an ancient civilization which had not learned to haggle with modern specie. When in 1882–1883 Spain let down the barriers of her isolation to permit trade agreements with France and Germany, violent protests were voiced among Spaniards that they had been duped and that the interests of their country had been sacrificed to the foreigners. Thereafter the motto of Spanish foreign policy became: "Friendship with all, intimacy with none."

The Profits of Neutrality

Spain fought for a place in the concert of powers, intrigued to be invited to every international conference where she was even remotely concerned, and strove to maintain the façade of her former glory. All the while, foreigners who acceded to these demands knew that behind the decorative portals there was no living power. Spain was regarded as the cadaver of a great nation, whose ghost, at appointed hours, stalked into European capitals, bedecked with the trappings of its ancient grandeur. Out of reverence for the past the rulers of Europe made a slight obeisance to the specter, this "historical expression." True, it was only a ghost, but it might come to life again; and in the delicate system of alliances and alignments of the epoch even a ghost was better as a friend than an enemy.

What friends could Spain have? France was a republic of radicals, an affront to the monarchical principle in Europe, an ancient enemy whose invasion under Napoleon I had never been forgotten. England was a carnivorous commercial animal which had consumed Portugal and now sought to devour Spain. Italy was irreligious and antipapal, the antichrist among nations, for it had humbled the spiritual father of Spain. Though Germany was powerful and willing, her manner was so overbearing that the proud Spaniard, with nothing to back up his pose, dared not become too intimate with the colossus. When in the early nineties Spain did toy with the Triple Alliance, her obligations were never determined and the extent of her commitments was never made public.[2]

Disinclined to support a European *liaison*, in 1898 the Spaniards, unaided and with the fatalism of men doomed to defeat, embarked upon the Spanish-American War. It was one of the most ludicrous episodes in modern history: the United States, a young nation, extending into Spanish territory its firm imperialist tentacles, swathed in idealism; Spain, with one of the worst-equipped navies in the world, defending a brutal regime of slavery established by her sixteenth century conquerors. Only with the turn of the century was a chastened Spain, definitively cut off from transoceanic colonial relationships, forced into closer economic contact with the great powers of Western Europe. England, France, and Germany came to consider Spain a semicolonial country, half-virgin soil for exploitation and investment. When prohibitive Spanish tariffs made exports impossible for foreign industrialists, they invaded the peninsula and established factories on Spanish soil. Thus from 1900 on the country enjoyed the general prosperity of European capitalism. While there were crises which temporarily threw Spain into turmoil—the Moroccan War and the anarchist uprisings of 1909[3] —the economic trend on the whole was markedly favorable.

This well-modulated economic development of Spain under the patronage of the European powers was violently affected and thrown out of gear by the World War. Straightway a mass of pamphlets, which vied with each other in depicting the cruelty of the Germans and the vices of the French, were let loose upon the country. To religious Spaniards, France remained a fountainhead of Jacobinism which imperiled the very existence of the Catholic church. A triumph for the Allies would mean a world inundated with revolutionary propaganda which might overflow the sacred dikes built by the clergy to safeguard the Spanish soul. The manner in which the anticlerical legislators of the Third Republic of France had persecuted the religious orders, and especially the Society of Jesus, could never be forgiven, not even after a concordat with the papacy had seemingly sanctioned these impious arrangements. No more could the English heretics at Gibraltar, a thorn in the side of Spain, endear the Allied cause to nationalist and devout Spaniards. In the opposing camp, Emperor Wilhelm, lord of the Central Powers, had never shown himself overgracious to his Catholic subjects, and for Spanish taste had all too often associated himself with the mission of Protestantism. Since his tyrannic lust for power seemed no less a danger to orthodox Catholicism than the spread of Anglo-French heresy, Spain could not identify herself with either cause. To be sure, the liberals, the writers, the lovers of culture, and the socialists were Francophile,[4] while the more violent and fanatical Carlists tended to be Germanophile;[5] but the mass of upper-class Spaniards shrewdly remained indifferent to the supposed ideals of the warriors and turned Spanish neutrality to profit.[6] Alfonso XIII played the role of the last humanitarian king on the Continent and spent his spare time arranging for the exchange of prisoners.

In view of the possibilities for official corruption inherent in the Spanish administrative system, the contemporary stories about secret aid to one or the other side in the conflict may easily be credited. On the whole, events create an impression of pro-German sympathy among the authorities. Tiny Spanish ports on the Mediterranean harbored German submarines which, when informed about the movement of French and English vessels from other Spanish ports, emerged to torpedo Allied ships still in Spanish waters. Barcelona factories manufacturing textiles and ammunition for the Allies were blown up by agents, reputedly German, whom Spanish officials allowed to escape with impunity. Evidence of this aid to the German cause was, however, not palpable enough to arouse official censure on the part of the Allies, and no one was startled when immediately after the armistice a new minister of foreign affairs, the Conde de Romanones, an outspoken Francophile, rushed to Paris to aid in the reconstruction of Europe.

Apart from the superficial modernization of her great cities and the role which Spanish diplomats played on the international scene as messenger boys for the belligerents, the four years of the war induced a profound transformation in the peninsula. Neutral Spain became a nation of profiteers. The results were not altogether favorable for her later economic existence. Industries established in haste with the purpose of rendering a maximum immediate output were destined to suffer the consequences of an artificial development in the postwar awakening. Nevertheless, in the twenties, even after the slump of 1921, Spain found herself in an economic position far superior to her prewar status. The war had given Spain an opportunity to tap her resources and to realize the extent of her latent economic powers.[7]

An Industrial Revolution

During the war the contending powers were driven to expend their energies upon products for internal consumption and to neglect their foreign customers. Moreover, the naval blockade increased the hazards of shipping to the point where commerce was no longer profitable. Spain, finding herself without a source for manufactured goods, was forced to make an economic *volte-face* and to change the predominantly agricultural nature of her productive system.[8] Both the Allied and the Central Powers, willing to pay even exorbitant prices for any materials which could possibly reach their supply bases, encouraged this transformation. Though in the later years of the war a sharp rise in the value of the peseta and ever more perilous shipping conditions seem to have restricted momentarily the purchases of the belligerents, Spain resumed her exports a few years after the peace settlement in order to provide for European reconstruction. Prior to 1914 Spain had been known in the markets of the world primarily for her fruits, wines, leather, wool, and canned vegetables; by 1919 the *Financiero* (July 4) could maintain that manufacturing had become the predominant factor in Spain's national economy.

There was a reversal of the monetary movement, which had drained the country in the sixteenth and seventeenth centuries. As the prices of her products rose steadily higher gold from the north of Europe poured into Spain. A negative trade balance of 247,420,000 pesetas in 1913 was by 1917 transformed into a positive one of 577,490,000 pesetas—a change which under existing circumstances was indicative of growing prosperity. The mining and manufacturing enterprises and the railway developments of the early twentieth century had been fostered by foreign capital. Now Spain could utilize her sudden prosperity to buy back the stocks and bonds and to reestablish her economic independence. The repatriation of a foreign debt amounting to about 590,000,000 pesetas was another sign of the new trend. By the end of the war only 310,000,000 were still outstanding, and these were partly balanced by 210,000,000 which the French had borrowed.[9]

When Spanish capital took to the creation of new companies for the exploitation of natural resources and industrial opportunities, the immediate gains were attractive to investors.

Fifty such enterprises in the Basque provinces and 294 in Catalonia netted rising profits with the following rhythm:

Year	Pesetas
1914	79,000,000
1915	34,000,000
1916	107,000,000
1917	209,000,000
1918	446,000,000

The mineral industry was outstanding for the variety of elements it could offer in the creation of a great industrial country. Mines, neglected because corrupt politics had placed insurmountable obstacles in the path of successful development, had long since awaited exploitation. When a local *cacique* obtained a mining concession by royal decree for one of his clients, the latter would rarely apply himself to a rational utilization of the grant with a view to long-term gains. He would instead seek immediate returns from the investment and would soon abandon the half-exploited mine for another. As a result of wild speculation only a relatively small proportion of the thousands of concessions awarded at random were ever exhausted. These handicaps, typical of a corroded political system, did not, however, prevent an increase in the total value of Spain's mineral production from 462,190,000 pesetas in 1914 to 1,387,100,000 in 1918.

During the course of the war coal imports, mainly from England, which had in 1914 amounted to 2,701,913 tons, fell to 465,447 tons, as the production of Spanish mines rose from 4,424,439 tons in 1914 to 7,537,822 in 1918. Mines in the Asturias, which since the late nineteenth century had been worked by English and French companies, produced a fourth of Spain's total coal extraction. The province of Vizcaya, with a fourth of the iron in the peninsula, became a great metallurgical center. Santander was noted for its zinc and lignite. Almadén in the province of Ciudad Real revealed the most extensive mercury deposits in the world. In Murcia there were both variety and abundance of ore—iron, copper, lead, and zinc. The Peñarroya coal mines in the province of Córdoba and the Rio Tinto copper mines near Huelva assumed steadily greater importance and came to figure in the speculative activity of financial interests throughout the world.

Nationalist pride, which had never before loomed as a significant factor in Spain's economic development because noblemen had disdained industrial activity, now appeared to hamper progressive industrialization. As long as manufacturing and commerce were not appreciated, the foreigners had been allowed free play with Spanish resources. Once there was some realization of their country's natural wealth, Spaniards were no longer willing to endure the foreign directors whom the industrialists of Paris, Berlin, and London appointed to supervise their Spanish branches. Spanish financiers, hesitant to invest in their own country, became none the less indignant at the intervention of foreign capital. In the last years of the war a movement of "emancipation" was initiated, marked by violent xenophobia. Spain was determined to become economically self-sufficient. Foreign engineers and factory managers were dismissed; outside capital was discouraged. In harmony with the new economic ideal was the repatriation of stocks in Spanish mining and metallurgical companies which had formerly been held by investors in other lands. Apart from soothing the injured sensibility of Spaniards becoming industrially minded, this movement, at its height, only disturbed production. In the beginning there was not a sufficient number of native technicians to assume the responsibilities of the foreigners, and the efficiency of many enterprises suffered. Exclusion of capital from abroad was soon found to be so disastrous that many of the early restrictions were removed.

Postwar Depression

The momentary rise in prices during the war appeased Spanish entrepreneurs, and they never strove to expand their internal market. When in 1919 the extraordinary requirements of the ex-belligerents ceased to nourish the industrial expansion of Spain, the lack of foresight of Spanish manufacturers was clearly revealed. The tremendous gains of wartime profiteering had by no means been allowed to seep proportionately through the lower strata of society. The purely speculative nature of much of this prosperity is indicated by a comparison of the accounts of the 50 great commercial and industrial banks, which rose from 535,000,000 pesetas in 1915 to 2,000,000,000 in 1918, with savings deposit accounts showing only a 50 per cent advance. In 1921, following a sudden slump in the demand for cotton and woolen goods from Catalonia, the Bank of Barcelona crashed. The mining and metallurgical establishments of the Basque country similarly declined, and bank failures in Bilbao, their financial center, shook the whole province. A reaction soon manifested itself over a broad area, even in the country districts, where stocked-up farm products and wines found no outlet. All the elements of a general depression made themselves felt—limitation of consumption, fall of wholesale prices, and restriction of credit. As early as 1920 the mass emigration of 147,918 souls paralleled the movement of 1914. And in 1921 the unfavorable trade balance of 500,000,000 pesetas signified return to the prewar pattern.

During the early twenties a number of Spanish industries betrayed their faulty organization in a chronic decline. When at the end of the war English coal, no longer needed at home for war industries, was allowed to reappear on the Spanish market, the Asturian operators discovered that they could not compete successfully with the product of a better-equipped industrial system. Their first move was to lower wages. Violent strikes followed. During the war, except for a shortlived and badly organized revolutionary movement in 1917, there had been comparatively little disturbance of industrial activity on the part of the working classes,[10] for employers who risked losing tremendous profits from even a short suspension of labor had readily acceded to demands for shorter hours and higher wages. In the postwar period strikes were common, and as they increased in number they often passed beyond the confines of economic dispute to assume a revolutionary character. Employers were usually ignorant of the ideological transformation of their workers in the limited areas where industrialization had become concentrated and intensified. Entrepreneurs envisaged the new labor organizations merely as riotous bands which would have to be suppressed by the Civil Guards. Cheap labor, the Spanish entrepreneur's only advantage over foreign enterprise, was about to be lost to him through militant strike action. The Asturian mine owners therefore stubbornly resisted the attempts of the workers to restore the war scale of wages, and they freely used the military police to enforce their will.

The iron-mines of the postwar period experienced an equally critical phase. In the year before the war, out of 9,861,668 tons

of metal produced, 8,900,000 tons had left Spain through the port
of Bilbao for export to England and Germany.   This quantity
had been reduced by a half during the World War, and the trade
had never entirely recuperated.   When England began to
suffer from a metallurgical crisis in 1921 the export from Bilbao
fell from 6,000,000 to 1,000,000 tons in a single year, another
factor in the general depression of Spanish economy in the early
twenties.

High tariffs appeared to be the only protection against foreign
dumping, a simple instinctive solution.   The policy was traditional in Spain and is typical of a regime where power is divided
among numerous groups, all of which must be appeased by concessions.   Tariffs became a subvention to mine operators and
manufacturers alike, and Spain was soon surrounded by the
highest tariff walls in Europe.   After having coddled nascent
industries, protectionism stifled any spirit of enterprise among
manufacturers; for there was no incentive to abandon old, costly,
and wasteful methods, and to introduce new techniques.   A rise
in the cost of living, a limitation in the consumption of manufactured goods, and privation for workers and peasants were normal
consequences.   The vast projects of an industrialist-financier like
Cambó of Barcelona were based upon the idea that within these
tariff walls Spain would build her own railways, harness her own
power, and develop her own harbors.   But no sooner had Spain
begun to effect some improvement in the means of communication, whose sorry state was the primary impediment to any
thoroughgoing industrialization, when Spanish capitalists grew
expansive and began to invest capital sorely needed at home on
the international market.   Criticized by economists for their
folly, the Spanish men of enterprise presumptuously proclaimed
that if internal industrial projects and international capitalist
ventures had not been found incompatible by the Americans and
the English, they saw no reason why they might not be similarly
successful.

In truth, there were neither competent industrialists nor a
favorable political framework for the elaboration of a "great
national economy," the term which had become the standard
feature of political orations.   When Spain experienced an
economic revival during the World War it might have been
expected that the Treasury, receiving an ever greater income

from divers sources, would have attempted to put an end to its annual deficits and to bring some order into the appalling state of public finances.   Economic transformation, however, had taken place within the old political system, one of whose fundamental tenets was the unwritten law that privileged groups could not be taxed.   From 1913 to 1920 the state did not increase its budget by more than 57 per cent, a subject for eulogies in contemporary newspapers, actually evidence of the government's unwillingness to develop roads, railways, irrigation, and seaports.

Furthermore, during the same period, the army, the navy, and "action in Morocco" were consuming an ever greater portion of the budget.   From 424,000,000 pesetas in 1917 the *soldatesca* annually increased its demands until it drained the Treasury of 1,195,000,000 in the fiscal year 1921–1922.   If the expenditures of the Civil Guard (the military police) are added to the ordinary accounts of the armed forces, their share amounts to 35 per cent of the total budget of the central government.   And since a large percentage of the war materials had to be purchased abroad, most of this expenditure was a total loss to Spanish industry and to the "great national economy" of the speechmakers.   Economists in their earnest simplicity stated that the condition of public finances would not permit extravagant colonial ventures such as the Moroccan expedition.   Though in 1918 the peseta had been so far above par that even the English pound was quoted at 19.86 pesetas instead of the normal 25.225, during 1921 Spanish money fell precipitously, and by August it had lost 34 per cent of its former value.[11]   It became clear that Spain would do better to expand her domestic improvement program than to seek glory in a conquest of the Riff tribesmen.   But considerations of this nature, countinghouse talk, had no bearing on the war councils of an army whose weapons were growing tarnished from disuse.

Capitalist Enterprise in Feudal Form

Backward as Spain was in accepting many modern techniques, one outstanding exception was the development of electric power —an example of Spanish potentialities in other fields.   In tiny communes there was a direct transition from oil lighting to the incandescent lamp; in factories, from animal to electric power. Since mechanization appeared late in Spain the most recent improvements were often available and whole stages in the history of industrialism through which other European countries had had to pass could be hurdled with a bound. At a time when fairly rich French municipalities were still hesitating about a change from gas to electricity, small towns in Castile had electric lamps in their little floorless white huts. The tremendous hydroelectric resources of the peninsula with its many swift-flowing rivers naturally fostered this development. The high price of coal and the difficulties of transporting it through mountainous country were further inducements to accept hydro-electric installation. It has been estimated that during the ten years after the war a capital of 2,000,000,000 pesetas was invested in the electrical industry. Little wonder that the future of electric power in Spain became the subject for sanguine reports at congresses of Spanish engineers and at world-power conferences.

Yet the internal contradictions among the social classes who ruled Spain prevented any concerted effort in the rehabilitation of the land. Modern industrialism, adorned with the *clichés* of nineteenth century liberalism, could not thrive in a petrified forest of feudal forms. Spanish industrialists were still haunted by the fear that productive activity was base in the eyes of the church and of the nobility. The aristocratic idler considered the manufacturer a low fellow, for conquest alone was the legitimate manner of gaining power. Even the great secular philosophers of Spain, outraged by the tinsel with which the *nouveaux riches* were specking the sombre image of their country, fostered this prejudice. Therefore the industrialist, as soon as he amassed enough wealth, hastened to buy lands or one of the castles of an impoverished noble. There was always something essentially speculative and even illegitimate in manufacturing, which had to be hallowed by the purchase of feudal property. And because industry was primarily gambling, the entrepreneur hesitated to re-invest his profits in the purchase of new machines, whose advantages would only be revealed with time. Since his profits were ill-gotten he preferred to live luxuriously rather than to accumulate riches, and periodically he had to wipe away the stigma by spending his money on such broken-down dukes and counts as sought his friendship. Only when he invested in stocks and bonds of foreign countries did he become a financier, less disparaged than an actual entrepreneur by nonproductive nobles. Therefore prominent Barcelona industrialists contented themselves with old machinery which had been repaired in England, while they speculated on the international market. Since human material was cheap, and the protective tariff was more than adequate, there was no incentive to improve capital equipment.

Sectionalism played its part in retarding the progress of industrialization in Spain. A few entrepreneurs might discuss plans for the reorganization of the whole of the nation's economy, but others would not subordinate even for a while their own regional demands to any general conception of an industrial Spain. The politicians who spoke for the great feudal landowners of the south fought the politicians who represented the industrialists of the Basque country and Catalonia. Further complications were set up by a struggle between the forces of heavy industry from Bilbao and sponsors of textiles from Barcelona. There was chaos when the banking interests in Madrid joined now with one side, now with another, disrupting the peaceful alternation of Liberal and Conservative ministries by the formation and dissolution of chance combinations and cliques. With every industry presenting a persuasive brief for its own protection, an impasse was the inevitable result. Coal operators from the Asturias, for example, demanded prohibitory tariffs. If they were raised high enough, English coal would be excluded and Spain would be constrained to rely upon her own coal supply, extracted under unfavorable technical and managerial conditions, hence exorbitant in price—an impediment to the progress of other industries. Should the country remain open to imported coal, Spain would become dependent upon the foreigners, and a native industry would be destroyed. Similar arguments were presented by various branches of industry and agriculture.

Observers agreed that Spain's industrial revolution hinged upon a solution of the transport problem. Spain needed a modern railway system with standard railway tracks so that trains from France would not be prevented from going beyond the border towns of Irún and Portbou by the Spanish narrow gage. The existing system had been constructed in accordance with.the dominant policy of centralization, all lines spreading out from Madrid to the industrial and commercial cities on the coast. When traveling from Algeciras to Valencia, for instance, it was first necessary to ride to Madrid and then to change for the

final destination.   For progressive industrialism it was imperative to build and to operate well-managed roads which would
join the productive coastal centers with one another.   Though
railway building in a mountainous country with numerous sharp
declivities was not so cheap as the construction of a road on a
French plain, men of foresight realized that none of the resources
of the country could ever be exploited until they made the initial
sacrifice.   An elaborate system of communications would open
an ever more expanding domestic market for the industrial
products of Catalonia.   There might even result a comparative
equalization of the standard of living throughout the peninsula.
Demands for manufactured products from millions of Spanish
peasants might turn factory-owners away from a frenzied attempt
to compete on the world market with more experienced industrial
nations.

Spanish industrialists, born into an old capitalist world leaving
little room for expansion abroad and surrounded by the debris of
a semifeudal regime at home, only toyed with such projects.   In
reality, lower wages alone meant profits to the entrepreneur now
and hereafter.   Foreign competitors had to be excluded.   When
conflicting interests harassed the central government with
demands for special privileges, all were granted in order to avoid
discrimination.   At a time when Spain should have been facing
crucial problems which concerned the very nature of her economic
system, the army, deprived of real war experience, was indulging
in an adventure against the Riff tribesmen of Morocco.   This
escapade added further to the strain of existing social and
economic relations and threatened to cause the breakdown of a
regime incapable of acclimating itself to the conditions of modern
industrialism.

A desperate monarch was given a new, though temporary lease
on his throne by the appointment of Primo de Rivera as head of
a military directorate.   But the dictatorship, for all its flam-
boyance, was only an interlude in the steady decline of Bourbon
prestige.

Notes

1. Albert Mousset, *L'Espagne dans la politique mondiale*, p. 32, Paris, 1923.
2. William L. Langer, *European Alliances and Alignments*, 1871–1890,
   p. 404, New York, 1931.

3. See Salvador Canals, *Los sucesos de España en* 1909, 2 vols., Madrid, 1910–1911.

4. Álvaro Alcalá Galiano, *España ante el conflicto europeo*, chap. 10, *Los "intelectuales" y la guerra*, pp. 189 ff., Madrid, 1916.

5. Don Francisco Martín Melgar, a Carlist, tried to counteract the influence of his party's standard attitude in *Germany and Spain*, London, 1916.

6. "To neutral Spain these problems mean little . . . , whether Russia grows in the occident and declines in the orient, whether Italy rounds out her territory . . . , whether Poland is resurrected, or whether Persia recovers her medieval grandeur . . . ." Dionisio Pérez, *España ante la guerra*, p. 192, Madrid, 1914.

7. On Spanish economy in this period see Mousset, *op. cit.*, chap. 19, *L'Économie espagnole avant, pendant, et après la guerre;* Jean Baelen, *Développement économique de l'Espagne de 1914 à l'avènement du directoire militaire*, Paris, 1924; the introductory section of Pierre Lefaucheux, *La peseta et l'économie espagnole depuis* 1928, Paris, 1935; Charles A. Livengood, *Spain; Resources, Industries, Trade and Public Finance*, Washington, 1930.

8. Dirección general de aduanas, *Import and Export Schedules of Spain*, translated by Blanche Bowers from the *Estadística general del comercio exterior de Espäna* (1916), Washington, 1920.

9. A. N. Young, *Spanish Finance and Trade*, Washington, 1920.

10. See Instituto de reformas sociales, *Informes de los inspectores del trabajo sobre la influencia de la guerra europea en las industrias españolas*, 1917–1918, 3 vols., Madrid, 1918–1919.

11. Lefaucheux, *op. cit.*, p. 7.

Chapter III

THE RISE AND FALL OF PRIMO DE RIVERA

For years after the Restoration of 1874 the *haute bourgeoisie* of Spain still vacillated between grand hopes of dominating the state and a secret dread of the unleashed elements of the proletariat, should a temporary upheaval allow revolutionary principles to be freely paraded. The Bolshevik Revolution of 1917, however, taught the Spanish middle class a graphic lesson. The pretensions of a few great Russian industrialists had brought them Kerensky, and Kerensky had opened the door for Lenin. Spain's bourgeoisie would be wiser; it would be contented with less profit, less grandeur, and fewer offices in the state. It would maintain intact the idols of the old regime, preserve the clerics and the warriors, and intimidate the masses; in return, its personal security would be assured in a turbulent world where the specter of communism had taken on flesh and blood. Even after the introduction of hydroelectric power plants, the Spanish middle class remained a modern appendage to a semifeudal system, for thus it hoped to save itself from all the ills to which capitalism was heir. "A living dog is better than a dead lion."

Having appeared late in the capitalist epoch, the Spanish bourgeoisie of the twentieth century could not mature into a successful revolutionary class in its own right; at the first symptoms of social and political disorder it might be relied upon to support staunchly the "feudals." Although the industrialization of the World War period had again held forth the prospect of a society in which the feudal landlords and spiritual mentors would occupy a subordinate position, the factory owners resisted the temptation. Terrified by the workers, they felt that Spain was far safer for them under the aegis of a minister of God—even though there was no God.

For the working classes of Spain the World War had brought new relationships and novel conditions of existence. Communication between cities and the countryside had been somewhat

38

improved.   There was a marked movement of population from agricultural districts to larger towns; provincial capitals reported far greater increases in the number of inhabitants than did country areas.   The normal attraction of the higher wages which accompany industrial revolutions was fast building up new urban centers.   Moreover, during this same period, the events of world politics were so striking that new ideas seeped through to the lower strata of Spanish society.

Workers in Revolt

Working-class ideologies long since planted in Spain burgeoned forth overnight.   Though the Bourbon Restoration of 1874 had declared the Socialist Party illegal, its first branch had been established in Madrid in 1878, and its program of union activity, its demands for the nationalization of property and for universal education had been proclaimed.   The Congress of Barcelona in 1882 had gathered representatives of 88 workingmen's unions; three years later the party organ, *El Socialista*, appeared.   The General Union of Workers (*Unión General de Trabajadores*), which by 1891 included about 60 branches, became the trade-union organization of the Socialist Party, its demands including trial by jury, universal suffrage, freedom of the press, recognition of trade unions, confiscation of church lands, the eight-hour day, minimum wage and child labor laws, the income tax, and that shibboleth of the German Social Democrats, a demand for the full product of a worker's labor.   In 1891 the Socialists had won a few municipal elections in the mining towns of the Asturias. These followers of Karl Marx, with their stable and centralized party authority, were, however, outnumbered in Spain by the anarchists, who opposed centralization and political action, and who had supported Bakunin at the Hague Congress of the First International.

Anarchist groups differed in various parts of the country, for there was local autonomy in each section of the party—indeed, freedom of action for each individual.   The syndicalists of Barcelona were notorious throughout Europe,[1] and stories about the revolts engineered by the Black Hand in Andalucía appalled organized society, though an almost complete lack of documentation makes it impossible to verify the tales which government authorities regularly spread about the plots and assassinations of this group. The Socialists, who believed in the efficacy of political action and in social reform, remained the inveterate enemies of the anarchists, and Pablo Iglesias, the revered father of the Socialist Party, exerted every effort to disassociate his followers from these working-class outlaws and their methods. Back in 1890 he complained that the May Day demonstration of the Spanish workers would have been far more successful "had not the anarchists, who are forever hindering the labor movement and the cause of labor organization, brought forward a proposal for a general strike."

As soon as news of the Russian Revolution spread over the peninsula, the workers in Spain became sanguine about the possibilities of a similar victory in their own land. Throughout 1917 the anarchists were constantly gaining in power and were sorely harassing the Barcelona industrialists. Then even their rivals, the Socialists of the General Union of Workers, ventured to become militant. On August 10, 1917, revolutionary strikes whose aim was the proclamation of a republic broke out in Barcelona, Madrid, Bilbao, Valencia, and Oviedo. Barricades were raised. Several hundred victims within a few days was the toll of the abortive revolutionary attempt. During this crisis the throne of Alfonso XIII was preserved by a loyal army which did not hesitate to use its machine guns. And in the years which followed the alliance of the monarch and the military came to play an ever more dominant role in Spanish history.

Alfonso XIII and His Soldiery

Alfonso XIII was an irresponsible braggart, a showy sportsman, a poseur on one of the loftiest stages in the world. When still a boy of sixteen, at the council of state which he unexpectedly called after his coronation, he betrayed a desire to personalize an ancient absolutist conception of government.[2] His ministers tried in vain to explain that since the Bourbon Restoration Spain had been a constitutional monarchy in which the king accepted their advice. Even though Alfonso had no well-coordinated political theory to guide his actions, he could easily make use of prevalent popular execration of corrupt parliamentarism to render his personal intervention in government desirable. The politicians wrangled on for years, passing grandiose laws; the hirelings of the same politicians, in administrative office, spent

their time in successful attempts to evade the new measures.   In
contrast to the crassness of the politicians, the sympathetic
manner of the King, even his frivolity, endeared him to many.
In a struggle between monarchical absolutism and the vicious
manipulations of the politicians, the latter could never hope for
any warm support from the people.   The Liberal and Conservative parties had lived on graft and intrigue; their preservation could hardly become an ideal.   Men would not die to
maintain the old *caciques* in power.

The army had a somewhat more complicated development than
its Bourbon monarch, and an understanding of its intervention in
Spanish politics at this period merits a digression.   When in the
nineteenth century political power in England and in France was
being wrested from the nobility, the bourgeoisie appeared with
a dove of peace.   The victorious class even developed a physical
characteristic, a certain portliness, which would demonstrate
beyond a doubt that it was incapable of bearing arms.   To
paraphrase Adam Ferguson, its eighteenth century apologist,
it pretended to inaugurate a civil society of commercial and
industrial peoples in contrast to the dying regime of noble
warriors.   The army lost caste in bourgeois Europe during the
comparatively "peaceful" nineteenth century, though the
degree of its fall was not everywhere identical.   In countries
such as England and France, where civil virtues insured pre-
dominance in the state, the army, powerful as it was, became
subordinate to the lords of finance and industry.   In Germany,
where the transition from the warrior to the industrial society
had been more abrupt, the military remained a rather independent
class.   Finally, in empires such as Japan no basic social transformation occurred; the army merely adopted the techniques of
industrialism without being tainted by its ideology.

Modern Spain, one of the most backward countries in Western
Europe, had not profoundly altered the character of her army
generals.   During the War of Independence and the subsequent
Civil Wars, *pronunciamientos*, and *coups d'état* Spain had come
to suffer from a hypertrophy of her military bodies.   So many
young people had been drawn into the armed profession that
during the rare intervals of peace which Spain enjoyed in the
nineteenth century most of the soldiers could not be absorbed in
other occupations.   Thus the ranks of the military establish-

ments swelled beyond the normal necessities of the land. The
military came to be accepted by tradition as an integral part of
the state organism and the administrative bureaucracy. It was
no longer a body primarily devoted to national defense or even
national conquest. Its duty was to preserve the government in
power, and hence, by a loose interpretation of this mission, to
alter a regime when it no longer harmonized with the army's
desires.

One of the causes of the native insurrections in Cuba, Puerto
Rico, and the Philippines was the brutal conduct of soldiers
who had been sent to the islands in great numbers because of
the congestion of warriors on the peninsula itself. After their
defeat in the Spanish-American War they returned in disgrace
and complicated further Spain's readjustment to the new economic conditions of the early twentieth century. The soldiers
were unpopular; there was a prevalent feeling that Spain would
not embark upon another military adventure. Joaquín Costa
ordered the coffin of the Cid to be sealed. The army sulked;
the generals found it difficult to maintain their morale, for, as
José Ortega y Gasset has expressed it, "no organism can remain
strong if the prospect of even future usefulness seems to have
disappeared."[3] When the mass of the Spanish people came to
detest and to disregard it the military, feeling itself ostracized
from the polity, conceived of an existence not only apart from,
but actually in opposition to other groups—politicians, intellectuals, and workers.

The armed forces were still identified with the nobility,
whose members were honored with advancement according to
the length of their pedigrees, not their technical competence.
The natural result was an army akin to the French military
establishment of the eighteenth century, top-heavy with officers
who did nothing. In 1909, when the Moroccan expedition was
undertaken in order to provide an outlet for the restless staffs
hoping to retrieve their honor in Africa, the Spanish army had
11,700 officers for its 80,000 men, a ratio of one to seven, which
should be contrasted with the French of one to nineteen for the
same period. Though class barriers in the army were not so
rigid as those of castes in their heyday and men did rise from
the ranks, the career general or the veteran of Moroccan wars
having overcome the prejudices of the nobility and won a promi-

nent position tried to ape the manners and opinions of those about him. His humble birth, far from arousing any sympathy for the lower classes, caused him all too often to exaggerate the reactionary sentiments of the noble army officers. General Sanjurjo, for instance, who was to have led the 1936 army rebellion had he not been killed in an airplane accident en route from Portugal, was of peasant origin.

The army in an incompletely industrialized country like Spain could not pretend to continue the conquistadorial traditions of its past into the twentieth century or to compete for world dominion with imperialist powers accoutred with massive mechanical weapons. In lieu of foreign wars, it turned its mind to the internal problems of the regime. As a field of exercise it had a narrow strip of territory in Morocco, where its generals could win medals for valor while suffering defeats in skirmishes with the wild tribesmen. At home the military had earned the gratitude of the upper classes because only the violence of the soldiers had in 1917 preserved the existing social system from revolutionary overthrow.

Civilian Politicians

Nonmilitary conservatives, the lawyers, the men of finance, and even the dignitaries of the church did not, however, relish army interference in the normal civil administration. Soon after the World War the Spanish church, fearful of the hegemony of the military, began to seek alliances in other camps. It showed the first signs of elasticity when it secured for itself representatives among all parties to the right of the rabid anti-clerical Republicans and Socialists. In 1921 the papal nuncio even sanctioned the formation of Ossorio y Gallardo's Christian Democrat Association, composed of 30 Catholic writers, who, taken together, had written 500 volumes on social problems.[4] The church of the early twenties, conscious of the new social ideas which had penetrated the masses, was testing the strength of various groups and was prepared to make limited concessions. As long as its own central power was not threatened, it was willing to bend to the right or to the left, so that during the intrigues and kaleidoscopic ministerial changes of Spanish post-war politics the princes of the church were not often found among the losers.

Conservative laymen never dared advance too boldly in undermining the army's power. Memory of the strikes of 1917, continued revolutionary rumblings among the workers, and more frequent anarchist uprisings in Barcelona never permitted the bourgeois to assume complete control and to reduce the army to the role of agent of national defense. The ruling classes preserved the army's prestige as a necessity of their own existence. The army in turn, cognizant of its indispensability, grew still more pretentious. Spanish generals fancied themselves as modern counterparts of Pizarro and Cortez, as conquerors unfortunately handicapped by the petty restrictions of capitalist civilization. And in reward for their suppression of the workers the army *juntas* were actually granted controlling power in the state. The Bourbon monarch himself subordinated attributes of divinity and sovereignty to his most prized title, which in his mind best expressed his true nature—that of first soldier in the kingdom. Though the leading conservative politicians in the Cortes were not always docile in the face of the extravagances of the military, the army could not be insulted with impunity. A Law of Jurisdictions dragged before a military tribunal any civilian who dared to cast improper reflections upon the army or its personnel. The integrity of the army was as indisputable as the dogmas of the Faith.

The army was not mechanized and its inefficiency was notorious. Since it had not been afforded the experiences which perfected other European war machines in the years 1914–1918, the long-drawn-out Moroccan campaigns were checkered with defeats. The swagger and bravado of the generals better expressed itself at banquets where warriors in their cups not infrequently betrayed military secrets. Nor did the soldiers blame themselves for their failures; these were easily explained as another crime of parliamentarism or of incompetent civil officials who surrounded the minister of war. Abd-el-Krim, the former employee of the Spanish civil service in Ceuta who joined the Riff uprising, knew all the weaknesses of his enemies and profited by them. Spanish arms were disgraced. "El honor" had long since vanished from the army, and wholesale graft and corruption in the purchase of supplies were rampant in the office of the quartermaster.

Alfonso XIII contributed his share in the movement to discredit the politicians in the Cortes, when he fostered discontent among would-be leaders of the two major parties, Conservatives and Liberals, whose orderly alternation in office had previously lent a semblance of stability to the regime. By sponsoring enough splinter groups the smooth working of the constitutional system, such as it was, would be destroyed. Since parliamentary majorities could be formed only by fortuitous combinations which were easily dissolved, no minister survived long enough to gain public confidence. Nothing nurtured antidemocratic sentiments more than the frequent recurrence of feverish ministerial crises. After 38 cabinets had passed in and out of office during a single reign, the people would welcome a dictator to displace the bungling ministers. There are indications that the King himself preferred the prevailing system of fast political change and its concomitant bewilderment, in the midst of which he could reassert his royal prerogatives in seventeenth century formulae.

The Moroccan Crisis

As soon as the social élite was endangered by the uprisings of the workers and the defeats in Morocco, the dominant clerical and militarist elements were loth to allow their monarch the luxury of political intrigue. The hesitations of the liberal cabinet ministers interfered with a policy of fierce repression in Barcelona; the civil and military governors of the same district were often at odds about measures of public order. Should Alfonso resist a dictator, the clergy and the military were prepared; if the revival of medieval doctrines of tyrannicide were inopportune, they could force abdication in favor of the heir apparent, still under age. The King was astute enough to forestall these treacherous manipulations, which had for some time been bruited about. When Primo de Rivera came the King was ready to press him to his bosom.

The conservative parliamentarians, sensing danger to their hegemony, had prepared a document on the whole Moroccan adventure, the Picasso Report. This was their attempt to humble—not to destroy—the growing power of the military. Evidence which was about to be presented before the Cortes in September, 1923, would have revealed the complicity of Alfonso himself in the disaster of Annual (1921). According to the documents, destroyed by Primo de Rivera as soon as he came into office but since gathered verbally from various members of the investigating commission, Alfonso had interfered with the regular processes of government. The warrior-king had privately goaded General Silvestre on to launch a grand offensive movement against the Riff without the consent of the minister of war, even without the knowledge of General Berenguer, the commanding officer in Morocco. When Silvestre's foolhardy gesture at Annual resulted in the most overwhelming defeat of a European army at the hands of natives since the Italian disaster at Adowa, a peculiar telegram from Alfonso was discovered among the effects of the General, who had probably committed suicide. It read: "Ole hombre—I'm waiting." This is the cry which the populace shouts at a bullfight in order to inspire the toreador to perform his most daring movements. The directness of this royal intervention was so bold that the parliamentarians were determined at least to chastise Alfonso for his extension of the manners of the arena to military affairs involving the lives of thousands of Spaniards.

The commission of inquiry hardly realized the serious implications of its charges and their possible consequences. Fatuous parliamentarians, they had been carried too far by the zest of their own debating, and they were about to disgrace their King-Father and his army, to reveal scandals which would provide material for the anarchist agitators. In their zeal to vindicate themselves they were proffering official documents to frantic mothers who had been asking why and for whom their sons were being sent against the wild tribesmen of Morocco. Women had laid themselves across railway tracks in Barcelona in crazed attempts to stop the departure of the transport trains. What might they do if the facts about the massacre of Annual were published? Should too many details of official corruption come to light, the whole social structure might crash. Sanctity would be torn from the church and nobility from the army. What could the moneylenders and war contractors expect as a saving grace?

The Directorate

The King-Father of a constitutional regime was not strong enough to survive the crisis. He needed a guardian angel or a major-domo or a dictator—and General Primo de Rivera came forward, pushed by a small army clique. On September 13, 1923, Alfonso submitted to the *pronunciamiento* of Primo de Rivera, the governor-general of Barcelona, and made him chief of a military directorate. The Cortes never met to hear the Picasso Report. The army in its own right, with the support of the King and the sanction of the church, "saved face" by driving the politicians from their debating society. The middle classes acquiesced, because after half a century of socialist and anarchist agitation they were frightened.

The Spanish dictatorship had thus not been preceded by the demagogic mass propaganda and violent demonstrations which Mussolini had staged to convince the forces of heavy industry, the Italian army, and King Victor Emmanuel that fascism was their only salvation. In Spain, where industry was even less developed than in Italy, it was not necessary to provide elaborate preliminaries. No appeal to the middle classes was required; an army leader advanced to preserve a social structure whose existence had been threatened by the incompetence of the politicians in the Cortes; and in this the army was fulfilling a traditional function. The standard type dictatorship known in Italy and Germany ground its way slowly, well-greased with pretenses to legality and to parliamentary form. Primo de Rivera had made an old-fashioned *coup d'état*, as befitted the status of Spain's economy. In 1926 the journalist Ramón Martínez de la Riva asked the dictator for some anecdote about the origin of the movement which led to power. The general laughed and exclaimed: "Hombre, the whole movement was anecdotal."[5]

The new directorate was at first conceived as a temporary expedient, invoked at a time of national emergency, and bearing a stronger resemblance to the ancient than to the modern Roman conception of dictatorship. Primo de Rivera had come for only 30 or 60 days. He stayed six years. . . . During his incumbency there were no serious uprisings and no violent strike waves. Foreign visitors, always impressionable, soon extolled the virtues of a regime which caused them far less inconvenience than any previous one had. Grand expositions at Seville and Barcelona bore witness to the thriving and prosperous state of the nation.[6]

Socialist Collaboration

On the face of it, the Rivera government's capacity to maintain itself in spite of revolutionary sentiments among the laboring classes is rather baffling. A brutal and thorough repression of the anarchists was partially responsible for the preservation of power. When Barcelona workers tried to resort to their old tactics, they were mercilessly beaten down; in celebrating the fifth anniversary of the dictatorship *La Nación*, the official government organ, could proudly contrast the prevailing civil order of 1928 with conditions in Barcelona for the year ending September, 1923, during which 337 workers and employers had been killed and 434 had been wounded in strikes and riots. But Joaquín Maurín suggests another reason for the directorate's survival in his incisive, though often erratic, *Men of the Dictatorship*,[7] written in the prisons of Barcelona and Bilbao during Primo de Rivera's regime: the participation of the Spanish Socialist Party, under the direction of the trade-union leader, Largo Caballero, and the professor of logic, Julián Besteiro, in the work of the new government.

According to Maurín's analysis, which bears some credence, the Socialist Party was willing to collaborate with Primo de Rivera because in 1923 it was on the verge of extinction. The anarcho-syndicalists, who revived their propaganda after 1917, had grown restless in their traditional spheres of influence in Catalonia, Levante, and scattered areas in Andalucía, and had begun to invade the Socialist stronghold of Madrid. When in 1920 Fernando de los Ríos, a Socialist leader and a professor of law, returned from a visit to Russia with an adverse report because Lenin had not sufficiently guaranteed the rights of the individual, the Socialist Party split into two factions, and one of them, henceforward known as the Communists, left to join the Third International. The old Socialist Party of Pablo Iglesias found its rule jeopardized by the Communists in the mining fields about Oviedo and in the industrial districts of the Basque provinces. Only the craft workers and small bourgeois elements of the capital thus remained loyal to the Socialists of the Second International. As a response to attacks launched against it, the Socialist Party, with university professors high in its councils, was not prone to outdo its rivals in violent revolutionary action. It was as likely to disapprove of the disorderly strikes of the anarcho-syndicalists as any upper class bourgeois, for such wanton disturbances were bringing its own pure ideology into disrepute with the many who failed to distinguish among the various parties of the Left. It cannot be said that the Socialist Party was blessed with outstanding leaders. Pablo Iglesias, a noble figure, revered by the socialist workers of Spain, was neither a profound theorist nor a powerful agitator. The party was reformist—not revolutionary—in the spirit of the mildest national groups in the Second International of the postwar period.

The Socialists had never before been considered a legitimate party in Spain because of their traditional and doctrinaire identification with republicanism. Now that their working-class ranks were being decimated by the onslaught of the anarcho-syndicalists and the communists, might they not abandon this republican fetish and collaborate with the monarchy and its new directorate? As the Spanish Socialist leaders surveyed the political activities of their brothers in other countries they found no apparent contradiction between monarchy and socialism. Had not MacDonald in England, Branting in Sweden, Stauning in Denmark, and Vandervelde in Belgium served their respective majesties?

If the Socialists accepted Primo de Rivera's call, they might as a reward be allowed to improve their trade-union organization and even secure the passage of enlightened social legislation. Hence the Socialists participated in the formation of Primo de Rivera's compulsory Boards of Arbitration, imported from Italy, which relegated the strike to the past epoch. In return for their submission the Socialist Party was granted some liberty of action: the publication of *El Socialista* was not stopped, and propagandists were allowed to move unmolested throughout the peninsula. True, there was something incongruous in this privileged position of the Socialists, granted by a dictatorship with which they must, theoretically at least, have been totally out of sympathy. As for Primo de Rivera, he never took his mission in life so seriously as his fellow-dictator in Italy, and the sensualist's levity and cynicism permitted the existence of many such anomalies in his regime.

When by 1929 the dictatorship began to wobble and Primo de Rivera planned to summon a farcical Constituent Assembly to bolster up his forces, the Socialists were not wholeheartedly opposed to participation, though their final vote was negative. Julián Besteiro advocated acceptance of the five seats which the dictator had graciously offered the party and attacked any attempt to preserve a "kind of unpolluted virginity" by abstention, for without governmental responsibility there could be no fecundity in action. But a far more serious offense had long since been committed by the Socialist Party; in the face of the imprisonment and transportation to penal islands of hundreds of anarchists and communists, it had allowed its trade-union leader, Largo Caballero, to sit in the Council of State.[8]

To the revolutionary workers this was a betrayal of their class ideals, and years passed before any *rapprochement* between the rival laboring class parties could be effected. The Socialist General Union of Workers had succeeded in maintaining its membership at about 220,000 throughout the dictatorship, and the Socialist Party had experienced an increase of membership from 5,395 in 1924 to 12,815 in 1929; men like Joaquín Maurín, however, could never accept the figures indicative of paltry gains as any justification for the official Socialist toleration of Primo de Rivera. Even a bourgeois republican like Álvaro de Albornoz, later minister of justice, was moved in 1927 to reflect on the Socialist policy in his essay *The cause of the worker and the cause of humanity (La causa obrera y la causa de la humanidad).* "In Spain," he wrote, " . . . the growth of the General Union of Workers has given Socialism a relatively strong numerical force. That handful of men who in days of struggle long ago gathered about the typographer Paulino [sic] Iglesias, the apostle with the harsh and strident voice, the rigid intransigent sectarian, is today a respectable organization." Don Álvaro was aware that, theoretically, Marxist phraseology was still in use, but "practically it [the Socialist Party] carries its opportunism to the point of no longer considering the form of democracy, that indispensable condition of all social progress, of any importance."[9]

If, in retrospect, the vital moral issue of this alliance between the trade union movement and the military dictatorship be overlooked, the result was not so unfortunate for the party as might have been imagined. Since the Socialists were the only political group, preferred above the Liberals and the Conservatives, who had been allowed to maintain their organization through the twenties, they were in a pivotal strategic position when Primo de Rivera fell. Endowed with an organization superior to any of the liberal parties, they were able, at the advent of the Republic, to exert a force far greater than their party numbers would indicate.

The Economic Policy

To justify its existence the dictatorship had to advertise its reforms. On March 5, 1929, in one of his official hand-outs to the press, the dictator reviewed his good works in the form of an *apologia:*

Peace in Morocco and within the country, personal safety, reduction of the term of military service, subsidies to large families, the creation of thousands of schools . . . , protection to agriculture, higher wages, social legislation, old age pensions and adequate establishments for the correction of delinquents, many and good roads, irrigation works, sanitariums, hospitals, dispensaries, sewerage, water supplies, dozens of bridges, modern armaments, powerful navy units, small increases in the income of the lower clergy and dependent classes such as widows and orphans of government employees or soldiers, appropriate establishments for our representatives abroad, treaties of commerce and of peace and arbitration—all these constitute an achievement which only a stupid people could fail to appreciate. . . .[10]

With the indispensable aid of the French, whom Abd-el-Krim had outraged, it was possible for the Spaniards to conquer the Riff, and a campaign which had cost Spain's weak economy $800,000,000 in 18 years was brought to a successful conclusion. The lives of some 13,000 men annually for ten years had been sacrificed to vindicate Spanish honor in Morocco. In administrative organization the dictator had once planned to purge the bureaucracy of officials who merely held sinecures, and he adopted circumspect measures in this direction. The cost of collecting taxes fell from 10 to 4 per cent of the total intake. Ordinary budgets were not only balanced but even showed a surplus of 2,000,000 dollars in 1927 and 30,000,000 in 1928. To be sure, the public works program, which made the regime so popular abroad, was not included in the ordinary accounts and had to be financed by a supplementary budget which revealed an ever-growing deficit. Since most of the public improvements like schools and highways were not destined to bring profits either in the near or distant future, there seemed little likelihood that the loans on which they were financed would ever be repaid.

Still, Primo de Rivera and his young Finance Minister Calvo Sotelo did everything in their power to give the appearance of orderliness and prosperity. The public debt was consolidated. A favorable trade balance was assured by one of the highest protective tariffs in the country's history. A National Economic Council was established to promote a variety of industrial projects which usually took the form of monopolistic concessions. The unattainable ideal of Primo de Rivera's finance system remained a peseta at par, a proclamation to the universe that the regime was sound. Unfortunately, even Primo de Rivera's Committee of Exchange with its fund of 500,000,000 pesetas could not defend the value of Spanish money against an attack of foreign speculators. When the distribution of petroleum, formerly in the hands of British and American companies, was taken over by the government, outraged foreign interests plotted a run on the peseta and revealed the essential weakness of the financial policy of the government. No decree could force the peseta up to par.

Fascist Paraphernalia

The economic difficulties of Primo de Rivera, though one of the direct causes of his downfall, might not have been immediately fatal had he, like other dictators, succeeded in building a political party about him. After the first year of the military directorate, there was an attempt to adumbrate the outlines of a fascist regime. During fraternal colloquies Mussolini and his king side by side with Rivera and his made an interesting quadruped for photographers. Cambó, the leader of the Catalan industrialists, was becoming ever more deeply impressed with the Italian formulae for the corporative state and had written a book on its structure.[11] The military police alone could not suffice to maintain a government in power; some popular base, however restricted, was essential for an enduring rule. Gesticulate as he might, neither Primo de Rivera's *somatens*, an imitation of Mussolini's fascist cells, nor his broad *Unión Patriótica*, presumably composed of all men of good will favorable to the regime, nor his motto—Fatherland, Monarchy, Religion—

aroused any widespread enthusiasm. He never formed a body
of Black Shirts with iron discipline. Mussolini's "theatre"
was a success; Primo de Rivera's feeble attempts to captivate
the people were considered an affront to the dignity of the ordinary Spaniard. Because he had without effort succeeded in
suppressing minor intrigues and abortive revolutionary plots,
Primo looked no farther. He was content with his wine, his
cards, and his women. After one nocturnal banquet he was
heard to remark if he had known in his youth that he was
destined to rise to power, he would have studied more and
fornicated less; now it was too late. This was truly a directorate
—as it was officially called—the reign of a libertine, a replica
of the days of Barras.[12]

Though Primo de Rivera was supported by his army friends
and by the church, and though he was tolerated by the timorous
middle class, he had by no means conciliated all factions, and
schemes were laid to oust him from power. These came to
nothing. Anarchist agitation was stamped out and revolutionary conspiracies such as the one concocted by Sánchez
Guerra in Valencia lacked popular appeal, limited as they were
to a small army clique and a few politicians.[13] Sánchez Guerra,
a leader of the Conservatives before the military *coup*, had been
minister of the interior during the strikes of 1917 and back in
1909 had voted for the execution of Francisco Ferrer. He
yearned for a return to the politics of the predirectorate—surely
no ideal to stir multitudes.

Far more threatening than such prematurely hatched conspiracies were the discontent and animosity smoldering in other
quarters. To the masses, perhaps, the Spanish state was
an organism which did not significantly impinge upon their
consciousness, for it made little difference whether they listened
to the blather of Sánchez Guerra or to the boasting of Primo de
Rivera and Alfonso XIII. Not so the intellectuals; they were
touched to the quick by events after 1923. For years before
the dictatorship, though they had endured the sneers of the
military and the scorn of the soldier for the clerk, they had
always been allowed to speak and to write. Primo de Rivera
frustrated the most overwhelming passion of Spanish intellectuals, the desire to be vocal. Through the first two decades of
the twentieth century the intellectuals had been allowed to pub-

lish their paradoxical reflections on life and death without serious molestation by royal ministers, too intent upon financial profit during their short terms of office. In the *Ateneo* the scholars and thinkers had gathered to while away their leisure hours, reading foreign reviews and exchanging utopian schemes for the reform of Spain.

Intellectuals, Conspirators, Revolutionaries

As long as they remained within the confines of this literary club in a building on a side street off the Plaza de las Cortes, their doctrines were as innocuous as the men who begot them. Before 1923 there was constitutional liberty in Spain and if the people were deaf to the informative discourses of the professors, one could not blame the King. The coming of the dictator transformed the intellectuals' natural ineptitude into martyrdom. Liberty was trampled upon. They were not even allowed to live in their own brainy wonderland. Hitherto the intellectuals had railed against local administrative impediments blocking the institution of reform; unless they turned into anarchist revolutionaries they could never have profound theoretical objections to a monarchy which allowed them all the ineffectual freedom they could desire. The dictator, by his display of repressive force, now moved the intellectuals to revive the libertarian phraseology of the French Revolution and the heroic republicanism of ancient Rome. By arming a censor with absolute control over all publications the directorate destroyed the very philosophic foundations of freedom. If a censor pondered long enough over a manuscript (which had to be sent to his office before publication), its timeliness would pass.

Miguel de Unamuno, a former rector of the University of Salamanca, wrote violent diatribes against Primo de Rivera and the King who supported the regime; it chafed him to be governed by an ignoramus. The vile bureaucrats, who could not even understand Unamuno's writings, allowed sharp criticisms to pass and wreaked their official vengeance upon some chance phrase which caught their eye. Humanitarianism and its implications had no part in the lives of these philosophers, but their intellectual dignity was outraged and they rashly joined communists and anarchists in their opposition to the debauched dictator and the monarch with his superficial *bon-*

homie. The material problems of earning a living, of food and shelter, which moved the anarcho-syndicalists and communists to revolt, meant nothing to the *idéologues* who exalted a few philosopher-kings above the rabble; but for the nonce they were all united in their hostility to the dictator.

Unamuno assumed a heroic pose and inveighed against the tyrant with passages from the classical literature which a professor of Latin and Greek knew well. For a while he was taken lightly by the dictator, who facetiously remarked that the philosopher imagined people should heed his political advice because he knew a lot of Greek. Unamuno was allowed many liberties. The monarch himself was often entertained by denunciations à la Savonarola, like an eighteenth century enlightened despot listening to the harangues of one of his *philosophes.* But, when the sage of Salamanca began to arouse popular interest and world sympathy, Primo de Rivera first held him prisoner on a barren island and then banished him to Paris. There a few students gathered about and he lectured to them in cafés—a low station for the former head of the University of Salamanca.

Don Miguel in exile became a symbol of the dictator's oppression, like Victor Hugo on the rocks of Jersey shaking his fist at Napoleon III. Soon Unamuno was joined by the popular novelist Vicente Blasco Ibáñez, whose *Alfonso XIII Unmasked* enjoyed a wide circulation in many countries. Their attacks tended to be personal rather than ideological. Ibáñez emphasized Alfonso's friendships with the proprietors of the gambling houses of San Sebastián and Cannes. He revealed that when M. Marquet opened a palace in Madrid for skating and less reputable pleasures, the monarch and his queen graced its inauguration with their presence.[14] . . . Though the eminent Spanish intellectuals aroused many sympathies in elegant French circles, the land of political refugees soon forgot them. The common hardships of exile made for strange companions. In the *Rotonde* in Paris the intellectuals deigned to meet with Spanish communists in a spirit of amity; the whole group even collaborated on a book, *España con honra* (*Spain with Honor*). These were romantic days of clandestine intrigue, when disaffected groups in the army, cast-off reactionary politicians mouthing hymns in praise of constitutionalism, and Andalucian lawyers met with wild anarcho-syndicalists to revile their common enemy.[15]

The professors who remained in Spain, less blatant in their pronouncements than Unamuno and his fellow-exiles, nevertheless performed a worthy function in spreading discontent among their students. When these began to organize strikes and to stage demonstrations the dictator was confronted with a troublesome element, because the students could more easily arouse bourgeois sympathies than could the workers.[16]

Berenguer: A Political Interlude

Primo de Rivera fell when his economic policies failed so dismally that even the timid Spanish industrialists abandoned him and joined their indignant protests to those of the intellectuals and the workers. The bourgeois elements began to fear that a further prolongation of the directorate might arouse a violent revolutionary movement of which they, too, would be the victims. Primo de Rivera protracted his term of office, and tried in vain to conceive of a dignified exit. With his customary lack of diplomacy he finally decided to poll the army generals and the admirals of the navy on whether he should remain in spite of the falling peseta and the rising discontent. Alfonso XIII, who by this time had come to realize his dictator's weakness and unpopularity, made an effort to extricate himself from the debris of the regime, censured the dictator for exceeding his authority, and demanded his resignation. Primo de Rivera, in disgrace, left for Paris in the last week of January, 1930, where he died a few months later.

The government of General Berenguer, which was then called into being, had as its purpose a return to some form of constitutional normalcy by which the King might be spared the fate of his dictator. The interlude was neither fish nor fowl; some oppressive measures were abrogated, others retained. When the only capable economist in Spain, Flores de Lemus, to save the peseta requested extraordinary measures on which the banks refused to cooperate, he bluntly posed the question to Berenguer: "Is this a constitutional regime or a dictatorship?" But there was no definite answer. The government was popularly dubbed the *Dictablanda* in contrast with the earlier *Dictadura*.

Official Spain was agitated with the problem whether the conservative politicians would forgive the Bourbon monarch for having violated his oath of office in 1923 and for having ousted them from power. Would they accept his regrets and aid in the convocation of a new Cortes so that Spain might return to the Constitution of 1876? On February 27, 1930, Sánchez Guerra, the hero of the fiasco at Valencia, delivered a most extraordinary public lecture at the Zarzuela Theatre in Madrid, to clarify their position. His speech abounded in platitudes. "To escape illegality, there is no other path but that of legality." His circumlocutions and evasions were no solace to the monarchy. "I am not a republican, but. . . . "[17] The predictatorship politicians, who had been ignominiously dismissed to make way for Primo, were hardly concerned with defending their sovereign. Sensing the general odium that was descending upon him for his part in the *Dictadura*, they rejoiced that they had found a scapegoat who might bear the blame for their own iniquities. They took refuge in an oratorical reconstruction of history and pleaded that their failures in 1923 had not been of their own making. They, innocents, had suffered because they had taken upon themselves responsibility for the misdeeds of others, to wit, the sins of the King by divine right.

When a political vacuum was created by the inability of the monarch to consolidate his position and to rally former courtiers about his throne, every conceivable group rushed in to seize power. José Ortega y Gasset coined a phrase: *Delenda est monarchia*. General strikes spread throughout the country. Catalan nationalism surged forward with a new breath of life and its representatives, meeting with a heterogeneous group of Madrid republicans at San Sebastián in September, 1930, swore to work in unison for the establishment of a new government. The Socialists offered the republicans their organization to provide mass support for the insurrection. The anarcho-syndicalists, with less ostensible collaboration, were no less prepared for revolution. Free-masonic influence in the army inspired hostility to the King because of his growing reliance upon the clericals. On December 12, 1930, occurred the first break: Captains Galán and Hernández, stationed at Jaca in the Pyrenees, decided to revolt, without waiting for the consent of republican leaders.   In a few hours the premature uprising was suppressed, and in spite of universal protest the officers were shot.   The revolution had two noble martyrs in the tradition of Riego, and Alfonso had once again stained his hands with blood.[18]   Republican leaders, Alcalá Zamora, an Andalucian jurist, Miguel Maura, the son of a famous prime minister, Fernando de los Ríos, a professor of law, Álvaro de Albornoz, a middle-aged attorney, Casares Quiroga, a young Galician lawyer, and Largo Caballero, secretary-general of the General Union of Workers, were imprisoned for signing a republican manifesto.

The Collapse of Monarchy

In 1931 Alfonso found himself alone, at the mercy of those same politicians whom he had abandoned in 1923.   Don Santiago Alba, the foreign minister in the last constitutional cabinet, who had been following events from his Paris apartment, refused a return engagement.[19]   Humiliated, the monarch called upon Sánchez Guerra, the former inmate of the Valencia prison. This practiced cabinetmaker began to plan the distribution of portfolios to Socialists, Republicans, Conservatives, and Constitutionalists, without prejudice.   He consulted Cambó, Alhucemas, Ossorio y Gallardo, Bergamín, Marañón, and—to provide a real Gilbert and Sullivan touch—the revolutionary committee which was holding court in the Model Prison of Madrid.   As for Alfonso, in the midst of these discussions he stayed in the Escorial "with the adored remains of his sacred mother," as the royalist historian has described him.[20]

When the Republican-Socialist combination refused the offer of portfolios in a monarchical cabinet, the King called upon Admiral Aznar—sea power where the land forces had failed. Disturbances in the universities continued, and unrest among the people was being fomented by the political parties.   The trial of the republican leaders who had been housed with dignity in the Model Prison turned into a festive antimonarchical demonstration; their six-month sentences were pronounced on March 23 and immediately remitted.   The revolutionaries were free to campaign for their candidates in the municipal elections of April 12, the day when the relative strength of all parties was to be tested conclusively.   On Saturday, April 11, there were parades of the unemployed in Madrid, and the marchers clashed with the monarchist legionaries as they passed the Nationalist Club. Representatives of the workers who appeared before Aznar demanded a minimum wage of two pesetas a day; their petitions were referred to the minister of labor. Propaganda meetings were held throughout the country; there was a sudden reawakening of political consciousness, for after an interval of eight years the people were to vote. They had matured to the point where it was no longer possible to "make" elections.

Results of the voting on April 12 began to be known the following day, and from early returns it appeared that in the country districts municipalities had remained monarchist. The cities, however, had reported overwhelming majorities for the republican candidates, and therefore, even before the votes were officially counted, the issue was settled, for none of the industrial centers would have allowed themselves to be ruled by the opinion of the "rotten boroughs" in the provinces. The revolutionary committee was gathered in Dr. Marañón's house to await the King's decision. The Conde de Romanones undertook to act as an intermediary between the monarch and the committee.[21]

At a cabinet meeting the King turned to his ministers for advice, and all except two of them voiced their categorical opposition to the use of force against the people. Alfonso XIII hoped for a month's respite during which elections to the Cortes, demonstrating the sincerity of his resurrected constitutionalism, could be prepared. But it was too late; towns throughout Spain were proclaiming the Republic. At Marañón's house the Conde de Romanones begged for a truce; when rebuffed he was willing to compromise on a regency with the Infante Don Carlos on the throne. Alcalá Zamora was adamant; the King had to abdicate unconditionally. Thousands of tricolors were being flown from the windows of the capital; confetti showered the streets.

Either to spare the blood of his people or to save his own royal head, Alfonso fled to Cartagena. There he boarded a battleship and departed for the race tracks of Europe.

NOTES

1. Royal Commission on Labour, *Foreign Reports*, vol. 9, London, 1892–1894.

2. Gabriel Maura Gamazo, *Historia crítica del reinado de Don Alfonso XIII durante su menoridad* . . . , 2 vols., Barcelona, 1919–1925.

3. José Ortega y Gasset, *España invertebrada*, pp. 78–79, Madrid, 1922.

4. Frank B. Deakin, *Spain Today*, pp. 56–58, New York, 1924.

5. Ramón Martínez de la Riva, *La España de hoy*, p. 29, Madrid, 1926.

6. The official record of the dictatorship and an exposition of its ideology were written by José María Pemán y Pemartín, *El hecho y la idea de la Unión Patriótica; prólogo del general Primo de Rivera*, Madrid, 1929, and *Los valores históricos en la dictadura española; prólogo del general Primo de Rivera*, second edition, Madrid, 1929.   More balanced accounts may be found in René Bec, *La Dictature espagnole de Primo de Rivera*, Montpellier, 1933, and Gabriel Maura Gamazo, *Bosquejo histórico de la dictadura*, 2 vols., Madrid, 1930.

7. Joaquín Maurín, *Los hombres de la dictadura.   Sánchez Guerra, Cambó, Iglesias, Largo Caballero, Melquiades Álvarez*, Madrid, 1930.

8. See Francisco Largo Caballero, *Presente y futuro de la unión general de trabajadores de España*, Madrid, 1925.

9. Álvaro de Albornoz, *Intelectuales y hombres de acción*, p. 230, Madrid, 1927.

10. Agnes S. Waddell, "Spain under the Dictatorship," *Foreign Policy Association Information Service*, vol. 5, p. 226, New York, 1929.

11. Francesc Cambó's work appeared in French as *Autour du fascisme italien*, Paris, 1925.

12. For a flattering character sketch of Primo de Rivera see Jérôme et Jean Tharaud, *Rendez-vous espagnols*, Paris, 1925.

13. Rafael Sánchez Guerra, *El movimiento revolucionario de Valencia*, Madrid, 1930.

14. Vicente Blasco Ibáñez, *Alfonso XIII Unmasked*, p. 65, London, 1925. Primo de Rivera's man, José María Carretero, caricatured the writer in *El novelista que vendió a su patria; o, Tartarin revolucionario*, Madrid, 1924.

15. Vicente Marco Miranda, *Las conspiraciones contra la dictadura*, p. 33, Madrid, 1930.

16. José López-Rey, *Los estudiantes frente a la dictadura*, Madrid, 1930.

17. César González-Ruano, *El momento político de España*, pp. 133, 137, Madrid, 1930.

18. See Salvador Sediles (a friend of Fermín Galán), *Yo voy a decir la verdad*, Madrid, 1931.

19. Santiago Alba, *L'Espagne et la dictature* (preface by Nitti), Paris, 1930.

20. Julián Cortés Cavanillas, *La Caída de Alfonso XIII*, p. 171, Madrid, 1933.

21. For the last days of Alfonso, see Conde de Romanones, *Las últimas horas de una monarquía, La república en España*, Madrid, 1931; Álvaro Alcalá Galiano, *The Fall of a Throne*, translated by Mrs. S. Erskine, London, 1933, and the closing pages of Melchor Fernández Almagro, *Historia del reinado de Alfonso XIII*, Barcelona, 1933.

Chapter IV

HALCYON DAYS OF THE REPUBLIC

Newspapers cried: "The dictatorship lasted for six years, three months, and seventeen days. Never forget it!" Their columns overflowed with bearded apostrophes to liberty and freedom, and their editorial pages ran with mellifluous phraseology. "The Spanish people must become master of their own destiny." More discreet journals resorted to euphemism. "Just aspirations of the proletariat must be protected." The press was capitalizing on the new regime, and the wealthy financiers who controlled it were netting tremendous profits from a suddenly revived interest in whatever reading matter was made available. The genuineness of this revolutionary enthusiasm may be surmised from the eclecticism of a man like Juan March: in the morning his *Libertad* was radical and republican, by evening his *Informaciones* (News) was monarchical.

Ambitious Andalucian lawyers like Alcalá Zamora and veterans of a dozen Alfonso ministries donned the Phrygian cap. Miguel Maura, who had intrigued with both the *Dictadura* and the *Dictablanda*, joined them. Instances of personal pique against the monarch have been advanced as explanations for these abrupt metamorphoses. But when the people of Spain opened their arms to all friends of democracy who might raise the nation from its moribund state, they refused to scrutinize past records meticulously. This was a new epoch; new vistas of democracy were opening before the dazzled eyes of the Spanish people; new souls were entering dry bones. The liberal optimism of the past century poured over the land like honey. Unmindful of contemporary Germany, the Spaniards cordially embraced the Noskes, the Eberts, the Scheidemanns—when they were not plagued with men of worse caliber.

Innocent exiles returned from distant countries to contribute their share of dithyrambs to the most peaceful revolution in the history of modern times. Gone were the days when the dynamite sticks of the anarchists and their pistols would be

61

necessary for the triumph of supreme reason. "Our Spain, in spite of the will of the butchers, has progressed." "The Pyrenees are no more"—an ancient echo for new Spain. The *leyenda negra*[1] of Spain shall be eradicated from the memory of man. We shall no longer be objects of amusement for a Gautier with his *Voyage en Espagne*. And vast changes shall be carried out with discipline. "Our legitimate enthusiasm will respect the bounds of the law," wrote Rodrigo Soriano, a life-long republican, as soon as he got off the boat from South America. "We, the reformers, are more men of order than they [the monarchists], because along with external order we seek the rhythm of order . . . , of spiritual order which is the true order."[2]

A mere proclamation brought the Republic into being, since the popular ballot had expressed itself only on candidates for municipal councils. When Alfonso XIII vacated the seat of power, he left behind him a document which specified that he had not abdicated; his royal rights were a trust for which he would one day have to render an account to God. Buoyantly the decree published by the Political Commission of the Republic attempted to glide over the technical difficulties of the situation; the statement had long been prepared, for most of the members of the Commission had been afforded an opportunity to discuss the minutest details of their first appeal while awaiting trial in the Model Prison of Madrid. "The provisional government of the Republic has assumed power without formality. . . . The people have elevated it to the position in which it now finds itself. . . . Interpreting the unequivocal desire of the nation the committee of political forces allied for the inauguration of the new regime designates D. Niceto Alcalá Zamora y Torres for the functions of President of the Provisional Government of the Republic." The proclamation was dated Madrid, April 14, 1931, and signed for the committee by Alejandro Lerroux, Fernando de los Ríos, Manuel Azaña, Santiago Casares Quiroga, Álvaro de Albornoz, Francisco Largo Caballero.[3] The Commission then proceeded to lay down the fundamental principles by which their temporary rule would be guided.

The Political Commission of the Republic

As a guarantee of democracy, they promised a review of their acts by the Cortes, when elected. They vowed to conduct a trial in order to fix responsibility for the uprooting of the parliamentary regime in 1923. They proclaimed liberty of conscience and religious freedom, and they recognized syndical and corporate personality along with the Rights of Man. They calmed perturbed spirits by announcing that private property was protected by the law and was never to be expropriated except for reasons of public utility, even then not before an equitable indemnity had been paid. Somewhat ambiguously they declared that the "agrarian law should correspond to the social function of the land." Finally, in view of the extraordinary circumstances under which the Republic had come into power, they assumed temporary administrative supervision over the Rights of Man which they had just granted.

Although there were marked similarities between the proclamations of Alcalá Zamora and those of the leaders of the French Revolution of 1830, a modern state could not become preoccupied with the subtleties of the problem of sovereignty, what it is and where it resides, much as the Spanish revolutionary lawyers would have been delighted by the debate. The issues were obviously social and economic. After years of pseudoconstitutional political maneuvering before 1923 and after the cant of the dictatorship, during which economic controversies had first been sugar-coated, then dismissed, the Republic was confronted with the task of providing a structure, or at least a framework, for a new social order. Indeed, the crisis of the nation's economy now seemed the more dramatic because its problems had been evaded for so long, and the facts had been covered over with the garish veneer of Primo de Rivera's speeches.

Though the new government had been ushered in by a peaceful and formal political revolution, the people were prepared to see miracles in the transformation of society; they were no less prepared to curse false prophets. The republicans were faced with the demands of labor, a disorganized army, the battle between religious belief and secular culture, starvation in agrarian districts—subjects which the poetasters of politics had played with for more than 30 years, pleas for reform which involved a complete reorganization of the social system. Most of the conservative republicans, however, who had mounted the revolutionary bandwagon, stagnated in a purely political universe of discourse. To them the Republic which had been pronounced without bloodshed was merely a constitutional novelty. The King had violated the law and he had been forced to surrender power. The law remained the Constitution of 1876 and as conservatives they would oppose any extravagant innovation.

Popular Decrees

The workers who had demonstrated so magnificently in the streets of Madrid and Barcelona and had maintained such admirable discipline during the revolutionary crisis were deserving of reward. Lest the masses pass from the holiday spirit of their public meetings to violent action and lest they stain the spotless escutcheon of the new Republic, special laws had to be promulgated without delay. The Socialist ministers of the new cabinet, Fernando de los Ríos, Indalecio Prieto, and Largo Caballero, were particularly instrumental in pumping a steady stream of popular decrees.[4] On April 22 the working classes of Spain were honored by a declaration that May first was henceforth a national as well as a proletarian holiday. Next, wage earners and soldiers were exempted from payment of the income tax, irrespective of their earnings. On April 28 it became obligatory for employers, when engaging agricultural laborers, to give preference to those resident in the vicinity of the commune where the work was being performed.

The right to evict small holders whose profits did not exceed 1,500 pesetas annually was strictly limited. As a fitting accompaniment to the celebration of the first republican May Day, the government unconditionally ratified the eight-hour day and forty-eight-hour week provision of the Washington International Labor Conference. To restrain agricultural proprietors from creating disturbances in the countryside by refusing to sow, communal boards were empowered to investigate what lands had been cleared and not yet worked. Provision was made to force landowners to give employment to the village laborers. Accident compensation was extended to agricultural workers. Associations of farm workers to lease holdings on a collective basis were sanctioned. An institute for the vocational rehabilitation of persons disabled in industry was established. To insure the health of painters the use of white lead and sulphate of lead was prohibited in interior work. On May 29 preliminary edicts were issued for the arbitration of labor disputes by officials of the ministry of labor.

Factions of the Cortes

With these new laws to guarantee the good faith of the revolution, the republican leaders could proceed to their main task, the convocation of the Cortes to frame a constitution. Since the temporary cabinet chosen by acclamation was composed of diverse elements it never pretended to act as a unified political party. The names of its members are worthy of record if only as a starting point for the strange and diverging paths which they were destined to follow in the next few years—though for the nonce they all toured Madrid in the same armored cars:

Provisional President and Prime Minister	Niceto Alcalá Zamora
Interior	Miguel Maura
War	Manuel Azaña
Marine	Casares Quiroga
Foreign Affairs	Alejandro Lerroux
Labor	Largo Caballero
Public Works	Álvaro de Albornoz
Post Office	Martínez Barrio
Justice	Fernando de los Ríos
Education	Marcelino Domingo
Finance	Indalecio Prieto
Economy	Nicolau d'Olwer

To assure itself a republican victory in the elections to the Cortes, this Provisional Cabinet ousted the monarchist candidates of the rural areas who had been victorious in the municipal elections of April 12, and placed republican appointees in control of local politics. Though this was a departure from legality, the consummate techniques of the *cacique* in swinging village elections justified such elementary measures of precaution. Thus on July 28, 1931, carefully organized elections rewarded their sponsors with an overwhelming victory for a Republican-Socialist coalition. Of their rivals, only a few agrarians, in reality disguised monarchists, and scattered independent conservatives who had achieved renown and popularity for their opposition to the dictatorship (Sánchez Guerra, Villanueva, Romanones, Unamuno, Alba, Ossorio) found seats.

Numerous factions within the triumphant Republican-Socialist coalition, held together for the moment by the fear of a monarchist *coup*, assured the new Cortes an animated existence. Only a few months of parliamentary life were necessary before these groups would cease to be indefinable republicans gathered about a chieftain, and would adopt distinctive policies. From the outset the following names were commonly used in the political press: Socialists (the most numerous faction), 116; Radicals (Lerroux), 92; Radical Socialists, 50; Progressives (Alcalá Zamora and Miguel Maura), 22; Republican Action (Azaña), 26; Republican Federalists, 17; Agrarians, 26; Navarrese and Basques, 14; Catalan Left Republicans, 43. One deputy, a lawyer, styled himself a "kingless monarchist in the service of the republic." In the midst of this parliamentary array two opposing influences were soon discernible: the Socialists, the most disciplined group, and the Radicals under Lerroux, who were often joined by the Progressives headed by Zamora. Early in the debates it was further evident that Azaña and his faction were exerting more power than their mere numerical strength warranted. Autonomous groups such as the Catalans limited their political pressure to regional problems.

One of the most ominous facts about the 470 members of the Constituent Assembly of 1931 was the large representation of lawyers, 123 of them. Jurists have ever been the curse of revolutionary assemblies, for though they may be imbued with the noblest ideals and may manipulate the most revolutionary phrases they usually think in terms of the old order. Their thought has become so warped by legal technicalities that any violation of procedure seems to be an infringement upon a personal right. In addition to the lawyers the Cortes of a nation of peasants included also the following occupations and professions: 65 professors and teachers, 41 doctors, 15 authors, 16 engineers, 3 architects, 8 ecclesiastics, 8 soldiers, 18 business men, 10 clerks, 24 workmen, 6 druggists, 2 veterinary surgeons, and 1 agricultural laborer. Since politics was not a vocation to most of the deputies they failed to attend the sessions regularly; their salaries were small and they had other professional duties. When bullfights were being staged in the Monumental Ring in Madrid the ranks of the legislators would shrink.

Intellectuals in Power

Alcalá Zamora, the provisional president of the Republic, now an exile in France because both sides in the present conflict rightfully consider him a traitor, has recently written a description of the Assembly. It merits full quotation because it is an unconscious caricature of one of the leading lights of this early period, of the Cortes itself, and of the values which prevailed among its members.

One must render the Constituent Cortes their due. The famous Cortes of Cadiz certainly did not have a greater love for justice, nor more generous enthusiasm, more devotion to their country, nor more respect for sincere adversaries than the Cortes of 1931. But they did not give birth to the same flowering of talents as the Cortes of 1869. It would be impossible to write about them a book like the one by Cañamaque [*The orators of* 1869]. Nevertheless, many times the discussion there was quite fine and certain speeches are worthy of figuring in an anthology of oratory.[5]

A great national uprising had elevated the lawyers and professors to power. Thousands had crowded into the Puerto del Sol to listen to their every word. They were naturally elated to find the whole people tendering them an homage which had been traditionally reserved for the military. We, the *catedráticos* (university professors), shall inherit the earth! We constitutional lawyers, logicians, professors of Roman law, psychiatrists, pessimist philosophers, half-poets, chemists, we are to be given control of this our beloved people, for whom we have always worked in our secret chambers, whom we have always loved in the innermost recesses of our hearts! Our schemes for social amelioration and the raising of the cultural level of the people will no longer be academic dreams and literary copy. . . . But once in the political arena, the professorial gladiators found it a more cruel world than they had ever dreamed. The combat was more bitter than their most heated academic meetings. There were hate, intrigue, personal ambition, class interest; there were coteries.

After long years during which they had studied profoundly, written sparingly and with insight, doubted at leisure, they were suddenly called upon to make decisions and to act with finality. Their days had always been pleasurably interrupted with *siestas*, long dinner parties, poetic discussions, reflections on

philology, life, death, and salvation, or the mystery of the
bullfight. Now their poesy and fine Castilian speech, their
psychological insights and fantasy, their knowledge of love and
their understanding of death were of no importance. They had
to work far into the night, and unaccustomed as they were to
such fatigue, they began to yearn for the old university chair.
Scholars and intellectuals who leave their writing desks for the
sake of the nation are apt to be soft fools, part-time revolutionaries. These men were often no more than political com-
mentators critical of existing conditions, who had longed to
act as well as to reflect, and in their mind's eye already imagined
the complimentary articles they would write about themselves.
A few months of the republican adventure had hardly passed
before Professor José Ortega y Gasset coined another phrase:
"The new regime has a sour and bitter profile."

The Framing of the Constitution

To expedite the framing of the constitution Ossorio y Gallardo,
a noted jurist, and an informal committee were requested by
the cabinet to prepare a draft since known as the *Ante-proyecto*.[6]
When the members of the Provisional Cabinet could not agree
upon a single one of the proposed articles of the *Ante-proyecto*,
they decided to leave the Cortes complete freedom of action.
Alcalá Zamora, the president, and Miguel Maura, the minister
of the interior, represented a degree of conservatism reconcilable
with the presence of their Socialist colleagues for no more than
the initial period of victory celebrations. It was settled that
after the Cortes debates each minister would vote independently
along with his own little faction. When the Cortes was convened
it rejected the document of Ossorio's Juridical Committee and
appointed a committee of its own. This new constitutional
commission was comprised of five Socialists, five Radicals, three
Radical-Socialists, two Catalans, one member of the Republican
Action, one member of the Republican Organization for Galician
Autonomy, one Federalist, one Progressive, one member of
the Club in Service of the Republic, one Vasco-Navarre deputy,
and one Agrarian (Gil Robles in his first disguise). On August
28 the group held their first sitting; and they labored so assidu-
ously that on December 9 the whole constitution was adopted
by the Cortes.

So many heterogeneous political elements were represented on the commission that the possibility of writing the document in the presence of all 21 members was soon dismissed. Grasping the initiative, the five Socialists, led by the talented journalist Araquistáin, meeting in a separate chamber, drew up a skeleton form for the constitution, with the understanding that the bourgeois republican elements in the committee and later in the Cortes would alter the draft. According to Araquistáin's own testimony in *El Sol*, the Socialists were truly surprised by the extent to which, after long discussions and numerous amendments, the basic principles of the original were preserved. The lack of unity in the final copy has been severely criticized by constitutional lawyers, the more subtle using their skill to discover contradictions between one article and another. Because of the frequent absences of deputies the color of the Cortes changed from time to time, and thus variations in the tint of its socialism left streaks on many constitutional articles. Wonder that the document holds together even as well as it does! The constitution reached a final vote largely because at this time republican leaders even in the most conservative groups, impressed by the peaceful ebullience of the masses, were eager to indulge in a few expansive generalities for the good of society as a whole. Although the Socialists had woven their ideological fibers into the constitutional fabric, most republicans were not unwilling to give lip-service to the new dogmas.

"Republic of Workers of Every Category"

The Socialists subjected the whole instrument to the criterion of the "socially useful" as contrasted with the abstract atomism and liberalism of eighteenth century constitutions. The fundamental problem of the document for the Right Republicans was somehow to limit the action of the state in its pursuit of these "socially useful" functions in order to maintain the essentially bourgeois tenor of the Republic. A hodgepodge of the Rights of Man with "socializing tendencies" was the result.

The very first article of the constitution is an excellent example of the potentialities of varied misconstruction which could be crowded into a single phrase. "Spain is a democratic republic of workers of every category (*de toda clase*)." This is a dogmatic statement not alien to the spirit of previous Spanish constitutions. The Cadiz formula of 1812 had specifically declared that it was the duty of all Spaniards to be "good and beneficent." The Weimar Constitution, which unfortunately exerted its muddled influence on more than one passage of the Spanish instrument, had similarly exhorted all Germans to devote their spiritual and physical capacities to the state. For the ordinary Spaniard this article of the constitution was an expression of disapproval with the *señorito*'s way of life, the hope of progressives that idlers, drunkards, gamblers, with and without titles, would no longer be deemed respectable citizens. The constitution explicitly censured the pretenses of the *jeunesse dorée*, who mocked industrial activity as ignoble; it longed for a productive and creative Spain.

The debates of the Constituent Assembly made it clear that the framers conceived of the first article in a Saint-Simonian sense, in the spirit of the early nineteenth century French pamphleteer who urged all men, irrespective of class, to abandon their internecine quarrels and to work. In an elaboration of Article 1, the Spanish constitutionalists pointedly declared that the activity of the banker, industrialist, astronomer, factory worker, and soldier were equally useful to the Republic. Nevertheless, the associations aroused by this phrase were such that its Marxian penumbra could never be entirely eclipsed. The "man" or "citizen" of the eighteenth century was here superseded by a new concept, popularly associated with the Soviet state, and the mere use of the word "workers" identified it with the language of class struggle. Hence in many translations and interpretations, the article was construed as if it had read "workers of all classes (*trabajadores de todas las clases*)." Reactionaries in Spain and other countries assumed that this was a recognition of social classes in the constitution, a provocation to class war. Leftist parties likewise loosely used the phrase as a sanction of proletarian democracy in their propaganda for advanced social legislation.

The Role of the Executive

The alternative of a "presidential" or "parliamentary" regime with all its implications was to be crucial for the later history of the Republic. In 1931, after the experience of the Primo de Rivera government, a strong executive who might usurp dictatorial power could not be popular; and yet the weakness and corruption of modern parliaments, which discredit the republican ideal, had not escaped the legislators. The more conservative groups hoped that the Spanish parliamentary system would be bicameral because of the supposedly restraining influence of the senate. Others wanted a council which would frankly represent organized social and economic interests, 50 workers, 50 employers, 50 representatives from autonomous regions, 50 professors, thus introducing into the democratic structure the much advertised virtues of the corporative system. It was the unformulated illusion of those who had presented their plan in the *Ante-proyecto* of the constitution that conflicting economic and social groups, provided with a chamber for discussion, would understand each other and would be less likely to engage in street battles. Brushing such conservative proposals aside, the Constituent Assembly decided upon a single body elected by the universal suffrage of all Spaniards, male and female, over twenty-three years of age. The nation was sovereign and the duly elected members of the Cortes were its representatives.

The president was not to be elected directly by universal suffrage, lest in some strife with the Cortes he point to a popular mandate equivalent to theirs. Instead, the Cortes and a special electoral body, meeting together, chose the president for a six-year term. Once elected, the president was expected to rise above political quarrels and to represent an abstract ideal. Out of its abhorrence of dictators, the Constitution of 1931 thus created a presidency with no vital powers, in a historical period which clamored for strong executives. "El Presidente" was the silent man and his functions were primarily ceremonial. He attended expositions and pressed buttons to raise curtains. Should the president intervene in the political quarrels of the Republic it would be considered an offense against the free play of parliamentary institutions.

Spain had deposed her king. As if to mock the "father of his people" and minister of God she put a puppet in his royal palace and surrounded a toy president with the tassels and the buckles and the military guard of the ancient monarchy. The French executive was the model. The Spanish Head of the State could not be interviewed by reporters, nor could he be quoted on any

controversial subject. The past alone was left open for him;
he could write his memoirs with a discretion worthy of his office.
Receptions, ambassadorial dinners, and the opening of art gal-
leries remained his particular province, for no one considered
banishing elegance and grand dinners and dress clothes form the
presidential palace. The president became the "social director"
of a country whose whole economic and cultural being was under-
going daily transformation.

One awful right was granted the president. Should the
parliamentary situation reach an impasse, he could dissolve the
Cortes twice within his own term of office. This practice of
presidential authority was not to be used too lightly because the
third Cortes, upon reaching its seats, would be called upon to
judge whether or not the second dissolution had been justified.
Should the third Cortes decide in the negative, the president was
to be removed from office.

The "government," as the Spanish constitution refers to
the prime minister and his cabinet, though appointed by the
president, needed a majority vote in the Cortes to remain in
power; thus was ministerial responsibility insured. The popular
assembly, ever jealous of its prerogatives, provided for a "permanent representation of the Cortes," based upon the numerical
strength of the various parties in the Chamber, to meet regularly
with the "government" during parliamentary recess.

Since this was a written constitution of the so-called rigid
type, a supreme court, called the Tribunal of Constitutional
Guarantees, was established to declare upon the constitutionality
of legislation. It was also empowered to arbitrate quarrels
between various autonomous regions, to act as a tribunal for the
review of presidential elections, and to serve as a court of justice
for the trial of the president, the prime minister and his cabinet,
the magistrates of the Supreme Court, and the attorney general
of the Republic. This body could only have revealed in time
whether it would usurp a position as pivotal as that of the United
States Supreme Court.

Property and Labor

The constitution was most up-to-date in its inclusion of
numerous articles actually prescribing the content of future
social legislation, for the deputies were not satisfied with mere

abstract provision for the intrusion of the state into new spheres. They described in detail the problems which required legal regulation. Divorce, legitimacy, and the protection of maternity were considered subjects for constitutional law. Most vital were the two sections which dealt with property and labor, since in them the "advanced" character of the constitution was clearly manifested. While countries with eighteenth century constitutions have been forced to interpret their documents broadly in order to allow for the elaborate paraphernalia of modern social legislation, the Spanish constitution laid down a set of general principles which might have led to some form of state socialism without the least infringement upon constitutional guarantees.

Article 44, on property, as finally adopted, reads:

The entire wealth of the country, whoever may be its proprietor, shall be subordinate to the interests of the national economy and affected to the support of public services, in conformity with the constitution and the laws.

The property of all kinds of goods may be the object of expropriation for the purpose of social utility, with provision for adequate indemnity, unless a law approved by the votes of an absolute majority of the Cortes makes another disposition.

Under the same conditions property may be socialized.

Public utilities and enterprises which affect the general interest may be nationalized when social necessity so requires.

The state may intervene with a law for the exploitation and coordination of industries and companies when the rationalization of production and the interests of national economy so demand.

In no instance shall the penalty of confiscation be imposed.

The language of this proposition, as originally phrased, had evoked serious dissent. Though the *Ante-proyecto* of the Juridical Commission had included a few of the same general concepts (not even the most conservative deputies, such as Castrillo and Gil Robles, defended the classic individualist ideal of property), it had been far more positive in its affirmation: "The state protects the individual and the collective property right." In sharp contradistinction, the draft adopted by the Parliamentary Commission, under Socialist inspiration, bluntly asserted that though the state recognized socially useful private property, it would "proceed to socialization in a gradual way."

Julián Besteiro defended this formula in the name of the Socialist Party, though he strove to emphasize that the socialization would merely be indicative of a tendency, a *criterio transaccional,* not the triumph of a Marxist principle.[7] The Parliamentary Commission's text was finally tempered, the result of an arrangement between the Socialists and the Radicals; these were won over only after it was specifically noted that any expropriation without adequate indemnity would require an absolute majority of the Cortes. The final formulation still left much to be desired, and logic choppers found numerous inconsistencies. A compromise between opposing parties which made possible the publication of a text in no wise harmonized fundamentally divergent property concepts.

Article 46, which deals with labor, is equally progressive and thorny:

Labor, in its diverse forms, is a social duty and will enjoy the protection of the state.

The Republic will assure each worker conditions necessary for a worthy existence. Its social legislation will regulate insurance in case of sickness, accident, unemployment, old age, incapacity and death; the labor of women and young people (*jóvenes*) and especially the protection of maternity; the length of the working day, the minimum and the family wage; annual paid vacations; the conditions of the Spanish worker in foreign countries; cooperative institutions; the economico-juridical relation of the factors which are included in production; the participation of the workers in the administration and profits of enterprise and everything that concerns the protection of the workers.

Those accustomed to eighteenth and nineteenth century instruments of government would never have imagined that such provisions were the stuff constitutions were made of. The novelist Pérez de Ayala, disturbed perhaps by the stylistic awkwardness of the article, proposed a briefer and more comprehensive formula, which the Cortes rejected; it insisted upon the detailed enumeration. Sophists were not wanting among the deputies, and they sharpened their pencils. After a protest on the part of Dr. Juarros the labor of "children" was excluded from the article and "youths" was substituted because obviously children would be at school, in accordance with a system of compulsory education which the Cortes was about to adopt.[8]

Church Disestablishment

Divergences of opinion, evident throughout the constitutional debates, flared forth with violence during the discussion of Article 26, which dealt with the regulation of religious orders.[9] The conservative *Ante-proyecto* had simply affirmed that there existed no state religion in Spain and that the Catholic Church was to be considered a corporation in public law. Should other confessions, it went on, seek the same status, the privilege would be awarded as soon as they presented proof of their substance. The Parliamentary Commission, which the anticlericals controlled, offered a text in quite another spirit: "All religious denominations shall be considered associations subject to the general laws of the country. The state may, under no circumstances, sustain, favor, or aid economically churches, religious associations, and religious institutions. The state shall dissolve the religious orders and nationalize their goods."

The ensuing debate over these contradictory proposals was marked by great bitterness and much oratory. Fernando de los Ríos, in no sense expressing the official sentiment of his party and merely speaking as an individual, offered a learned and subtle analysis of the essence of religion. Not a practicing Catholic himself, he was profoundly moved by what he considered religious feelings, and he expressed misgivings about the intransigence of his own party's stand. Amendments from the Right and from the Center then bombarded the Parliamentary Commission, attempts to mitigate the violent measure against religious orders. A compromise was proposed. The Socialists, meeting as a party, refused to agree to the new formula and sent Jiménez de Asúa, president of the Parliamentary Commission, into the Cortes to defend the original text along with a telling emendation: "The establishment of religious orders on Spanish territory is prohibited."

Though Jiménez de Asúa, a professor of law, undertook the task without much enthusiasm, he stressed many fine points during his parliamentary performance. Referring to the "exquisite elegance" with which the revolution had been achieved in Spain, he reminded the deputies that this peaceful attitude was possible only because the people expected firm resolutions from their Cortes. The church, by openly supporting the dictatorship, had intervened in a field which was outside its province.   Freedom of religion was safeguarded in Spain, for the Socialist proposal was not intended as an attack upon private conscience.   The speaker paid his respects to the religious feelings of others, but he saw no reason why unbelievers should contribute to the church in any form, since "Spanish Catholics are rich and many of them are part of the plutocracy."   When Catholicism was the state religion, the government placed vast properties in the hands of the religious orders as a trust.   Now that this relationship was broken the goods of those orders had to be returned to the state.   The argument that many monks were devoted to an other-worldly ideal and led a contemplative life bore no weight with Jiménez de Asúa, for thereby they were violating the article of the constitution which had declared Spain a Republic of Workers.   Neither was he impressed by the services which the religious orders had rendered in caring for the sick.   Mockingly he appealed to the doctors of the Cortes to testify to the pernicious influence which nuns exerted upon irreligious patients in the most crucial moments of life.

Jiménez de Asúa was followed by Manuel Azaña, who, though he spoke in favor of the compromise, was most dramatic in his emphasis of its frankly anticlerical connotations.   He announced that the new formula, without any intent at circumlocution, referred to the Society of Jesus.   Even though this were a breach with the liberal principle, the dissolution of the order was imperative because the presence of its members would frustrate any attempt to further secular ideals.   It was here that Azaña made the momentous pronouncement: "Spain has ceased being Catholic."

After a session which lasted all night until 6:35 in the morning of October 14 the following clause (Article 26) was finally adopted by a vote of 178 to 59:

All religious confessions shall be considered associations subject to a special law.

The state, the regions, the provinces, and the municipalities shall neither maintain, favor, nor provide economic aid to churches, religious associations, and institutions.

A special law will regulate the total abolition, within a maximum period of two years, of the state's budgetary allotment for the clergy.

Those religious orders shall be dissolved whose statutes impose, besides the three canonical vows, another special vow of obedience to an authority other than the legitimate authority of the state.   Their goods shall be nationalized and devoted to purposes of charity and education.

The other religious orders shall be subject to a special law to be voted upon by the Constituent Cortes in conformity with the following principles:

1. Dissolution of those which, by their activities, constitute a peril to the safety of the state.

2. Inscription on a special register of those which remain, subject to the supervision of the minister of justice.

3. Inability to acquire or maintain, by themselves or through intermediaries, more properties than those which, according to a previous account, are destined for their maintenance or the direct realization of their proper ends.

4. Prohibition to practice industry, commerce, or teaching.

5. Submission to the tax laws of the country.

6. Obligation to present to the state, each year, an account of the use of their properties in relation with the purposes of the association.

The properties of religious orders may be nationalized.

The passage of Article 26 of the constitution had thrust into the open fundamental contradictions within the cabinet. Alcalá Zamora, the president, and Miguel Maura, the minister of the interior, resigned on October 13 because this act of open hostility to the church and of militant anticlericalism violated their consciences. The ardent Catholics of the Vasco-Navarre deputation were so deeply outraged that they refused to sit in the Cortes with blasphemers and absented themselves for the remainder of the constitutional debate. It was a major crisis; if it were unresolved, the very existence of the Republic would be endangered. The Cortes went into permanent session and after the customary wrangling Manuel Azaña, who had just served as the leader of the anticlerical attack, emerged as prime minister. Henceforth there could be no doubt about the religious complexion of the Spanish cabinet.

Antagonism to Article 26 served as a rallying point for "clericals" and conservatives who were seeking an issue that might have some popular appeal. Relations between the officials of the church and the Republic. had from the beginning been strained. The confetti had no sooner been swept away from the streets of Madrid in May, 1931, when the Catholic Royalist newspaper *A.B.C.* heaped insults upon the new-born Republic, and Dr. Pedro Segura, the Primate of Spain and Cardinal-

Archbishop of Toledo, in a pastoral letter called for a unification of Catholic forces in defense of their interests.   Monarchist clubs dotted Madrid, and clashes occurred near their premises.   The people were on the alert to avenge insults to republicans from haughty ex-nobles, and as a result of one of the encounters a riotous spirit surged throughout the capital.   On May 11 the buildings of the *A.B.C.* were attacked.   A Jesuit church on the Calle de la Flor was burned.   Numerous incendiary incidents occurred throughout the south—an expression of the antagonism of the people toward ostensible symbols of past oppression, a warning to the enemies of the Republic that a grim fate awaited them.   To animate further the conflict, Cardinal-Archbishop Segura was officially expelled from Spain, and the new Spanish ambassador to the Vatican was not received.   Though other Spanish bishops publicly made conciliatory moves, the rumor and the reality of secret antirepublican propaganda from church sources fanned hatred.

Article 26 in its final formulation was a bludgeon held over the heads of the religious orders.   The discretionary power which it granted the government was an attempt to intimidate the church into accepting republicanism.   If other religious orders altered their ways they might escape the fate of the Jesuits. To many religious Spaniards, on the other hand, the measure was a call to martyrdom.   Even men with almost indifferent religious outlooks, like Alcalá Zamora, could announce that they were prepared to devote the rest of their lives to its revocation. From a secular republican viewpoint, the method thus pursued in undermining the influence of the church was unfortunate. The provisions injured Catholic sensibilities without immediately and efficaciously destroying the church's means of counterattack.   The final edict against the Jesuits was not passed until the next year; the other orders remained in an ambiguous legal status.   The enemy had been humiliated, not crushed.

Revolutionary Strikes

Equally serious attacks were leveled by the extreme Left upon the Republican-Socialist coalition, thus placed in the unenviable position of suppressing opponents on two fronts. After a few weeks of republican rule, the anarcho-syndicalists and the communists resumed their strikes and agitation.   The dictatorship had ruthlessly suppressed all attempts on the part of the workers to improve their economic status; it was natural, then, that the advent of the Republic should have let loose a series of strikes whose demands were primarily economic. The Socialists, who had assumed the responsibilities of power, were placed in a dilemma. They begged their members to be patient and they exerted their influence over the Socialist General Union of Workers in the hope that the workers would grant the government a breathing spell during which great reforms might be passed.

While for the most part they were successful in restraining their own adherents their pleas could not seriously alter the conduct of the Anarchist Federation, the Syndicalist National Confederation of Labor, and the Communists (members of the Third International or independent Spanish Communist factions). The militant revolutionary groups had only recently seen the Socialists in the council of the dictator, and they refused to draw fine distinctions between the more and the less radical elements in the cabinet. To them the government represented the capitalist system, and any petty reforms it might achieve were futile. The revolutionary parties were prepared to take every advantage of the liberties offered by the new Republic in order to disseminate their partisan propaganda. They would call strikes in order to win immediate gains for the workers— hoping to transform the strikes into revolutionary manifestations, if the moment were auspicious. They would take advantage of the bewilderment in the ranks of the Republican-Socialist coalition to hasten the tempo of the revolution. The anarchists awaited the day when they could proclaim their ideal society, without money and without a state apparatus; the Communists, the dictatorship of the proletariat.

Immediately after the municipal elections of April 12, 1931, the Communist Party had issued pamphlets and circulars in order to dispel "republican illusions" among the masses. The Communist leaders in cities such as Seville organized meetings and published as their program:

1. Agitation in all workshops and in all parts of town for the election of delegates who shall form the local soviet.
2. Arming of the proletariat.
3. Distribution of the land by the workers' and peasants' councils.[10]

Attempts were made to raise the red flag; it was torn down by the Civil Guard and partisans of the Republic; there was bloodshed. The membership of the Communist Party was negligible, however, because official repression under the dictatorship had almost completely eradicated its influence. In December, 1930, there were 14 members in Madrid; by April, 1931, about 200. The party was isolated and persecuted, and its leaders saw enemies lurking without and within. "The Communist Party has to fight not only against the bourgeoisie and social fascism but also against the Trotskyists and anarchists." On May 11, after the riotous clashes with the monarchists, when a state of martial law was proclaimed in Madrid, the Communists voiced their bitter dissatisfaction with the policies of the new government. "The big landed estates have not been touched, nor have the estates of the church been confiscated; the living conditions of the working class have not been improved." Largo Caballero was labeled a "social fascist," then a frequent epithet in Communist diatribes.

And indeed, Caballero's attitude toward the Barcelona manufacturers who came to complain about strikes was most conciliatory. "In my eyes," he said, "such action [the strikes] was just as unpatriotic as the emigration of those who take their capital with them in order to boycott Spain. . . . The working class, which cannot abandon its demands once the Republic is firmly established, must in the meantime consent to a truce." When strikers resorted to violence, the Civil Guard was called out; workers were shot down; scores were arrested. On July 20 a general strike in Seville broke out after a worker had been killed in a riot. "Civil War in Seville, 22 killed and hundreds of wounded are among the victims of the new bourgeois-social democratic Republic," wrote the correspondent of the Comintern's organ. On July 23 Largo Caballero further antagonized the revolutionary syndicalists and communists by announcing the introduction of compulsory arbitration. "Those workers' organizations which do not submit to it," the minister had tersely announced, "will be declared outside the law." On August 7 the Russian newspaper *Pravda*, expressing the official Communist policy, bore the following editorial: "It is true there exists practically no difference between the present regime of the republicans and the social-democrats and a military dictatorship. The

Civil Guard—the select gendarmerie of ex-king Alfonso—is proceeding ruthlessly against the workers. . . . The Spanish capitalists and landowners have no reason whatever to complain of their republican and 'socialist' ministers."

Strikes among agricultural workers and city laborers were organized now by one federation of labor, now by another; they were rarely coordinated; hence any revolutionary *putsch* could be nipped in the bud. Whenever the anarcho-syndicalists ordained that the Great Day had dawned, the police seemed better informed about the details of the revolution than most of the workers. The syndicalist trade-union federation, for instance, would call a strike without the sanction of the anarchist political federation; a local union, or a group of unions in a city might issue strike orders without the benediction of the central body of the trade-union federation or the governing body of the a-political F.A.I. (Anarchist Federation of Iberia). The possibilities for independent action were similarly numerous in the Socialist trade-union group. Irresponsible strikes were less likely only in those few unions controlled by the Communists because there a more rigid organizational discipline prevailed. With so much antagonism among rival proletarian organizations the strikes could never become the demonstrations of a strong or well-knit labor movement; they remained an amorphous expression of the desire of the working classes to force a more revolutionary course upon the government.

But what could be the achievements of the bourgeois-socialist coalition? Industry was refractory, unwilling to cooperate. Could a few men at the helm of the state forcibly regenerate the economy of Spain and improve the conditions of the laboring masses when the great industrialist elements remained stubbornly recalcitrant in the midst of an economic crisis? As mass criticism of the coalition's comparative neglect of urgent problems grew more vigorous, the cabinet emitted ever more proposals, and the Cortes interrupted its constitutional labors to sanction them. On June 24 an inquiry was planned into conditions of labor in the mining fields; on July 4 provision was made for the reemployment of those who had been dismissed during the railway strikes; on July 30 employment bureaus for agricultural workers were established; on August 28 the coal miners were awarded a seven-hour day, though other miners (ores) were still to work eight hours until the end of the year; on September 23 a bill ordering the compulsory tillage of land for reasons of public interest passed the Cortes.

Azaña—The Image of the Republic

When Azaña took office on October 15, after the ministerial crisis over Article 26, decrees became more forceful in tone. Lest an uprising on either the Right or the Left interrupt the labor of the Constituent Assembly, the new prime minister secured the passage on October 22, 1931, of a Law for the Defense of the Republic, which loaded upon the minister of the interior and the civil governors of provinces dictatorial powers temporarily abrogating the numerous rights and privileges guaranteed by the constitution. According to its provisions newspapers could be suspended indefinitely; meeting places and clubs, political and otherwise, could be closed; citizens could be imprisoned without recourse to *habeas corpus*. They could be forced to change their domiciles, or constrained to reside in given places within the national territory, or deported to Spanish possessions beyond the mainland. Industrial enterprises could be seized. Public meetings could be prohibited, fines could be imposed up to a maximum of 10,000 pesetas, civil servants could be dismissed. The law, which was later incorporated into the constitution, was decreed to be effective for the duration of the Constituent Cortes unless otherwise ordained by this body itself. The vast powers granted by the Law for the Defense of the Republic could not, however, be exercised so arbitrarily as many of the reactionaries who felt its sting have protested. It was always possible to appeal to the cabinet, and with ministerial responsibility the Cortes was really the final judge of the legitimacy of any extraordinary punishment. Nevertheless, the law, which was used to deport dangerous reactionaries such as Dr. Albiñana, sent to desolate Las Hurdes, or to suppress Communist newspapers such as the *Mundo Obrero* (*Worker's World*), did not strike the democratic character of the new regime into relief.

By the end of the year 1931 the halcyon days of the Republic had passed. Manuel Azaña was at the head of a coalition of Left Republicans and Socialists intent upon imposing their view of the constitution on Spain. The Radicals under Alejandro Lerroux were fast shying away from the coalition and soon joined the opposition along with the Progressives of Alcalá Zamora and a motley group of Republicans who grew constantly more agitated by what they denounced as the "Socialist dictatorship."

Manuel Azaña had come forth as the man of the hour, leader of a Republic of the Left. Born in Alcalá de Henares in 1880, he was an archtype of the frustrated middle-class intellectual, who before the advent of the Republic had languished in an obscure government position.[11] After receiving his early education from the monks in the Escorial he denied them when he reached manhood, and he refused to go to confessional again. He became the avowed enemy of their system of teaching, the more acrimonious because he knew their secrets. In his novel, the *Garden of the Monks* (*El jardín de los frailes*), which has been compared to James Joyce's *Portrait of the Artist as a Young Man* because of its soul-searing analysis of a young Catholic who has lost faith, Azaña left the record of his feelings toward the disciplinarians in whose hands had rested the molding of Spanish youth.

Once in a position of power he was determined that no other Spanish boy should be forced to endure a similar regimen. Steeped in Spanish tradition as he was, he had also acquired a universal culture. He had studied law; written dramas; translated a French collection of negro poetry and George Borrow's *Bible in Spain*. Like all underpaid government employees he had been forced to accept subsidiary occupations; he was General Secretary of the Institute of Comparative Law and Professor in the Academy of Jurisprudence and Legislation. His brilliant conversation had made Azaña one of the outstanding figures of the *Ateneo*, and he had been elected its president. The practical bases of state power had absorbed him as deeply as *belles-lettres;* he was the author of a book on French military policy, and his technical knowledge of military affairs had won him the ministry of war in the first cabinet of the Republic. Here was that extraordinary combination of the contemplative soul and the man of action. If a few weeks before the outburst of the military rebellion on July 18, 1936, one had followed Manuel Azaña, President of the Republic, at an exposition of modernist painting in Madrid, one would have heard the most refined comments as he passed from one work to another.

Cabinet Ministers

By Azaña's side in the cabinet of December 16, 1931, reorganized after the resignation of Lerroux, were three prominent Socialists. Indalecio Prieto, long a party member, was a bulky fellow with a tremendous capacity for work. He was witty, even Rabelaisian, a great mass orator. As a newspaperman in Bilbao, his party loyalties did not stand in the way of acquaintanceship with many leading Basque industrialists. Though he had once served his apprenticeship as a stenographer, this self-made man lived to see more prosperous days and to control *El Liberal* of Bilbao, making it his personal organ. While he was nominally a Socialist, Marxism as a dogma or even guiding doctrine had little meaning for Prieto. He was an ardent nationalist, who sought to encompass the economic regeneration of his country in order that all its inhabitants might enjoy its fruits.

As minister of finance in the first cabinet, he had striven to maintain some balance in the Treasury in the face of the economic and political crisis which had thrown normal relations out of gear. He was forced to report to the Cortes a budgetary deficit of 500,000,000 pesetas. To finance the social reforms and the new services which the Republic planned to install greater revenue was necessary, just when growing industrial and agricultural unrest had actually reduced the government's income. The railway budget sapped the resources of the Treasury, since traffic was considerably diminished and the new roads which Primo de Rivera had opened were running at a loss. The peseta was falling. In the new cabinet Indalecio Prieto was given the task of directing the ministry of public works and solving the unemployment problem.

Francisco Largo Caballero retained the ministry of labor which he had held in the first cabinet. He was a former stucco worker who had risen to be secretary-general of the socialist trade-union movement. Primo de Rivera had invited him to sit in the Council of State, and with the consent of his party he had accepted. He was known as the monk of the Socialist Party and was revered by its members as the successor to Pablo Iglesias, its founder. The position he occupied in the cabinets of this period made him the choice target for the revolutionary anarcho-syndicalists and communists, who spurned his "reform-ism" and collaboration with bourgeois republicans. In 1931 he had already reached his sixtieth birthday, and a kidney ailment gave rise to many rumors about his inability to endure the arduous labors which were imposed upon him.

Don Fernando de los Ríos, who in the reshuffling of cabinet posts had passed from the ministry of justice to that of education, was certain to cut as graceful a figure in one office as in another. His black beard, melodious voice, soft eyes, meticulous manners, all revealed an extraordinary sensitivity, which at times appeared almost precious. His socialism was romantic and Christian. He had been the Socialist Party's emissary to Soviet Russia soon after the Bolshevik Revolution and he had reported unfavorably on the new regime. The rights of the individual, he had found, were not being safeguarded sufficiently, and Lenin had been too preoccupied to discuss this defect in the Soviet system. For a professor of law (Fernando de los Ríos had held a chair at the University of Madrid), the ministry of justice was a fitting post. As a nephew of Giner de los Ríos, the founder of the Free Institute of Education, the ministry of public instruction was his by right. Don Fernando was no Marxian materialist, and *aperçus* about the soul of Spain flowed readily from his pen. He has been pictured most acutely by the reactionary Giménez Caballero—"a man who could be sent to any world congress, the Sunday-coat of Socialism." Throughout his political career the university remained his first love, and workers have naïvely described his discomfiture when he was thrust among them on some of their more festive occasions.

Six other members of the Azaña cabinet, who may be loosely classified as Left Republicans, were less striking personalities. Marcelino Domingo in the ministry of agriculture was considered a translation of M. Edouard Herriot into Spanish. He seemed to sum up all the paradoxes of a representative of the middle classes who is carried away for one moment by the revolutionary *élan* and the next moment turns about to preach discipline and order. Giralt was a chemist, an honest republican and a friend of Azaña's; he occupied the ministry of marine. Álvaro de Albornoz, an aging lawyer, moved along with the current and was a capable minister of justice. Casares Quiroga, a Galician fiery with a consumptive's intensiveness, it was said, had sacrificed his fortune to the republican cause. As minister of the interior it was his duty to maintain public order. Carner, a solid Catalan, was placed in charge of the finance ministry. Zulueta, an intellectual who along with Pérez de Ayala and Dr. Marañón had founded the Club for the Service of the Republic, was made foreign minister, and he drew upon this group for so many of his ambassadors that wits grew malicious about the Republic in the Service of the Club.

The Inauguration of the President

To grace his Republican-Socialist coalition, Azaña, with the fine hand of a seasoned politician, found a President whom even the London *Times* sanctioned.

There had been reason to fear that Alcalá Zamora, the Andalucian lawyer who had headed the original revolutionary committee and later become the first prime minister of the Republic, might emerge as the leader of a party of diverse elements coordinated on the basis of their common hostility to the anticlerical articles of the constitution. An ex-revolutionary opposing the republicans in power on grounds of conscience would make far too attractive a figure-head for any party. Hence Azaña rendered Zamora innocuous by exiling him to the presidency and by offering him an annual salary of 1,000,000 pesetas to ease his suffering. Zamora did not resist, and he was elected with 362 votes. Thus was the potential antagonist turned into a silent chief, as provided by the constitution. Scattered votes for the presidency were cast for Cossío, the venerable art historian; Unamuno and José Ortega y Gasset each received one vote, evoking reasonable suspicion as to who marked the ballots.

On December 11 the inauguration took place before the Cortes. Julián Besteiro, its president, a Socialist and a professor of logic, administered the oath. Then Alejandro Lerroux, an old revolutionary and anticlerical whose principles were fast changing, hung the glittering gold and enamel collar of the Order of Isabella the Catholic around the neck of the new President of the "Republic of workers of every category." The ceremonies over, Zamora drove off in one of the gilded coaches which had formerly belonged to Alfonso XIII. Moorish cavalry, sappers, and silver cuirassed guards passed in review. Four hundred thousand copies of the 125 articles of the constitution well-bound in substantial red, yellow, and purple covers were dropped from the skies by the aviation corps.

Ever true to their a-political preconceptions, the anarchosyndicalists refused to recognize the day as a public holiday; they presented themselves at their regular jobs, demanding either work or wages. On that day, in Gijón and Saragossa, a number of workers were killed in clashes with the Civil Guard.

Notes

1. Julián Juderías, *La leyenda negra. Estudios acerca del concepto de España en el extranjero*, Barcelona, s. a. (192?).
2. Rodrigo Soriano, *La revolución española*, p. 241, Madrid, 1931.
3. Adolfo Posada, *La nouvelle constitution espagnole*, p. 89, Paris, 1932.
4. The activity of Spain in this sphere during the first year of the Republic far exceeded any other country, as may readily be seen from a listing of the decrees in the *International Labor Review*, vol. 24, *passim*, Geneva, 1931. The texts appeared on the relevant dates in the *Gaceta de Madrid*.
5. Niceto Alcalá Zamora, "L'élaboration de la constitution du 10 décembre 1931," *Revue d'histoire politique et constitutionelle*, vol. 1, pp. 24–25, 1937.
6. For a history of the debates which centered about the Constitution of of 1931 and for an analysis of its text, see Luis Jiménez de Asúa, *Proceso histórico de la Constitución de la República Española*, Madrid, 1932; Posada, *op. cit.*; P. Marland, *Les principes de la constitution espagnole de 1931*, Paris, 1934; Carlos A. d'Ascoli, *La constitution espagnole de 1931*, Paris, 1931.
7. Jiménez de Asúa, *op. cit.*, p. 294.
8. *Ibid.*, p. 299.
9. For the parliamentary debates on Article 26 see *ibid.*, pp. 183–216.
10. For the Communist attitude toward the Republic during this period consult the reports of the party correspondents in the *International Press Correspondence* for 1931.
11. See Giménez Caballero, *Manuel Azaña*, Madrid, 1932.

Chapter V

THE SUBSTANCE OF REFORM

The year 1931 had ended ominously with an encounter on December 31 between the Civil Guards and the peasants of the village of Castilblanco in the province of Badajoz. The rancor of the peasants toward the military police who protected the landlords had expressed itself with wild cruelty. In the ensuing weeks the anarchists of Catalonia afforded the Republican-Socialist coalition no respite and forced Azaña to invoke the Law for the Defense of the Republic time and again. The January uprising in the Llobregat Valley precipitated brutal military suppression. Without allowing for a peaceful interval, monarchists and clerical reactionaries joined to harass the government on its other flank with plots and conspiracies. Though the cabinet was responsible to the Cortes, frequent recourse to extraordinary measures and special decrees gave rise to accusations of dictatorship. Early in March, 1932, a deputy exclaimed in the Chamber: "The shadow of Mussolini has appeared in our midst!" Azaña, however, was undaunted by the cries of tyranny, and when hard-pressed, he replied drily: "But I am not a liberal."

The Republican-Socialist government, backed by an ample parliamentary majority, was determined to pass a set of laws which would, within a short period of time, raise the framework of that regenerated Spain for which the constitution had already laid a foundation. To dismiss the Constituent Cortes at the beginning of 1932, as the Radicals demanded, would have left the country with mere formulae for future reform. Power was in the hands of a self-conscious group of middle-class Republicans and reformist Socialists, acutely aware of their historical role, imbued with a profound feeling for the social functions of the modern state. They had been well-fed on historical analogies, and they knew the story of the Girondins, of Kerensky, and of Madero. In bold defiance of the fate which had overwhelmed their political prototypes they resolved that a strong, instead of

88

a vacillating, Centrist policy should save Spain from the horrors of both revolution and reaction. Azaña was as powerful a Kerensky as ever has been called upon to fulfill that thankless historical mission. In the years 1931–1933 he made a valiant attempt to fashion Spanish economic and social reality in a Republican-Socialist image.

Reorganization of the Army

Unlike other "clerks" in a similar governmental position, Azaña appreciated the vital importance of the army in the political pattern. He himself took the portfolio of the minister of war and, among his first acts of legislation, initiated measures to reform the whole military establishment—thorough enough in nature to convince the generals themselves that their premier was no novice in these affairs. It had never been the custom in Spain, as in other lands, to reintegrate a good portion of the army men into the normal social structure; instead, new posts were being created for the officers, bureaucratic positions in some branch of government service where they would be permitted to retain their military rank. An extraordinary burden on civil society in time of peace was the consequence. In February, 1931, there were in the service 1 captain general, 18 lieutenant generals, 48 division generals, 128 brigadier generals, a total of 195 generals, aided by 16,926 officers. In the reserve forces were enrolled 29 lieutenant generals, 114 division generals, 414 brigadier generals, and 9,755 officers.[1] And with every increase in numbers the army lost its effectiveness. "In Spain," Azaña expounded to the Cortes on December 2, 1931, "we got to the point of having 22,000 officers for 16 divisions, and since there were no men for these officers to command we had infantry regiments with 80 soldiers and cavalry regiments without horses; a most picturesque situation was created by Primo de Rivera when the cavalry was divided into three sections, regiments A, regiments B, and regiments C. Regiments C did not exist; regiments B had half their official number; and regiments A had a theoretically effective number which never seems to have been reached in practice."[2]

To alter this absurdity the new minister of war, aiming at efficiency rather than numbers, reduced the military forces of Spain to eight regiments. Spain was given a fighting army of

151,000 men and the superfluous generals and officers were cautiously eliminated. Since it would not be safe for the regime to sack without ceremony all the unwanted generals and minor officers and thus create a dangerous group of malcontents, Azaña, with what he considered a master stroke, offered full pensions to those who would voluntarily present themselves for retirement. To the amazement of tradition-minded Spaniards, about two-thirds of the officers took advantage of this generous proposal, and overnight their number was reduced to 9,836. Though this transaction obviously cost the Treasury many millions of pesetas at the time, according to the estimates it would ultimately save 650,000,000 pesetas. The fact that the immediate drain might be catastrophic was never thoroughly realized. The army had to be won over to the Republic. Since other items of the army budget as debated in December, 1932, still totaled 387,000,000 pesetas, the reduction of expenditures from the dictatorship's requirements amounted to only 31,000,000—the 122,000,000 pesetas for pensions were of course reckoned separately. Nevertheless the emphasis of the budget differed decidedly from the days of the Moroccan venture, most of the expenditures being devoted to the improvement of the mess, the construction of new lodgings, and the purchase of modern technical equipment.

According to the new plan of short-term military service it was calculated that in ten years Spain would be ready to call upon 1,000,000 men for defense purposes. Noble-minded as it was to proclaim in the constitution that the new Spain outlawed war as an instrument of national policy, the fact was that no country could rely on the League of Nations for protection. Since an army was necessary, reasoned Azaña, let it be one of the best-equipped in Europe. When the effects of this great military reform tied up only about 10 per cent of the total government revenue, the minister of war felt justly proud. The parade of the soldiers of the reorganized army on April 14, 1932— the first anniversary of the Republic—yielded fulsome praise from foreign observers, who were duly impressed with the progress of the new military establishment.

Unfortunately neither the pensions nor the new discipline transformed the normal class sympathies of the army officers. A year of republican existence had not passed before the generals began to meddle in politics once again. Retired officers had greater leisure for intrigue than ever before; and men who scoffed at civil officials with the lofty disdain of heroes could not be intimidated by a threat that their pensions would be cut off. Company banquets became the occasion for minor political demonstrations as provocative allusions to the Republic were allowed to slip into the toasts. Even when the government arrested a few of the suspected generals, transferred and demoted others, the temper of the army was not altered. On the contrary, the arrest and incarceration of soldiers by civilians went far to outrage officers accustomed to the blanket Law of Jurisdictions, which had once bestowed upon them the right to tyrannize over those who wore no uniforms.

At a banquet of the military cadets in June, 1932, General Goded, Chief of the General Staff, in a speech replete with hostile insinuations made his point sure by shouting: "*Viva España!*" instead of "*Viva la República!*" at the end of his toast. The usual arrest followed. Such minor incidents of military disloyalty piled up and became one of the chronic threats to the existence of the Republic; for when generals were punished, those who remained untouched felt their brothers' wounds and smarted under the injury to their profession—insults delivered by professors, clerks, and lawyers. The antipathies between the army officers and the Republican leaders soon grew so violent that generals who had once been notorious for their Masonic affiliations—most of the leaders of the present rebellion—began to form alliances with reactionary groups in the church. Azaña had treated the malignant military cancer; he had not stopped its growth.

Statutes of Autonomy

The army was still in the process of reorganization when the Cortes was called upon to solve the problem of Catalonia. Catalan autonomy sentiment had created another issue for the reactionaries to dramatize, in its propaganda value inferior only to the church settlement. "Do not dismember Spain!" became the cry of the traditionalists. Even the Republican-Socialist coalition in power was not disposed to surrender to the Catalans absolute control over taxation and the school system.

Catalan separatism had been nurtured for many years on the fact and fancy of the historical outrages perpetrated against

Catalonia by the centralizing monarchy of Castile.[3] In the Middle Ages intrepid Catalans had built up a great empire whose outposts extended to Greece and Asia Minor. Union with the Castilians became the standard cause of Catalonia's decline. The destruction of Barcelona commerce in favor of Seville, which in the sixteenth century had been granted exclusive privileges for trade with the New World, cut perhaps the deepest wound. Once the economic demands of 2,800,000 people, owning one-fourth of the wealth of Spain, were warmly clothed in the colorful vestments of modern nationalism, the Catalan problem became the Spanish equivalent of Home Rule for Ireland.[4] In 1914 Alfonso XIII, hard pressed by the separatists, granted Catalonia a measure of self-government, an autonomous administration known as the *Mancomunidad*. Ardent Catalans craved independence and spurned such half-way measures. Hence in 1923, when confronted by ever more pretentious Catalan demands, Primo de Rivera abolished the whole system. Hatred for the dictator who had forbidden the use of their beautiful tongue, together with a desire for economic emancipation, prompted the Catalans to join with the Republican intellectuals from Madrid in the famous Pact of San Sebastián (September, 1930) which presaged the overthrow of the monarchy.

On April 13, 1931, a day before Alcalá Zamora's political committee assumed office in Madrid, the Catalans, somewhat impatient with the Castilian revolutionaries, proclaimed a Catalan State. It required all the grace and tact of Fernando de los Ríos, who was forthwith despatched to Barcelona by the Madrid chiefs, to restrict the Catalans to the terms of the original San Sebastián agreement, and, pending further constitutional provisions, to accept the status of *Generalitat*. In August, 1931, the Catalans passed upon a statute of their own formulation with one of the most overwhelming majorities recorded in modern times on any issue. The veteran Catalan leader, Colonel Macià, hastened to lay this document before the Cortes in person, and there it remained untouched until the following May. The Catalans were really aiming at a loose federation of Spanish peoples, each province with equal rights, to end at last the hegemony of Castile. They demanded exclusive jurisdiction over education, justice, and the police power; to the central government they were willing to surrender only limited privileges of taxation and the higher courts of justice.

The discussions which the Catalan statute of autonomy provoked both in and out of the Cortes were heated and scholarly. No matter how immediate a constitutional subject might be the learned ministers of the government could always preface their argument with a page of medieval Spanish history—when not constrained, as on the church question, to hark back to the Council of Nicaea. In a famous speech Premier Azaña explained that he was happy to restore to the Catalans the "liberties" of which they had been robbed in the days of Isabella the Catholic. His oratory flowed so profusely in the last days of May, 1932, that the Catalan deputies were overcome with emotion and the stenographers were exhausted. Turning to the Right Azaña maligned not only contemporary monarchists, but the monarchy of the most glorious period of Spanish history. Reactionaries could endure no more; they wept over the defamation of Spain's past. The autonomy statute was made an issue throughout the country. Patriotism was at stake and historians were at a premium in party circles. When discontent with the proposed *Estatuto* assumed concrete form, the Catalans protested against the numerous modifications which the Cortes was introducing into their original text. Extreme Catalan nationalists, the group which published *Nos Altres Sols (We Alone)* and would accept nothing less than absolute independence, were preparing a summons to rebellion.

As the debate dragged on over each article, the reactionaries, from Lerroux to the extreme Right, exerted themselves to rouse public opinion against the statute. Thousands were gathered into the great bull ring in Madrid to hear the orators intone patriotic phrases and bewail the dismemberment of Spain. Macià, the President of the *Generalitat,* a former separatist now content with autonomy, and his counsellor Lluis Companys, who had often defended anarcho-syndicalists at public trials, were the bogies of Madrid conservatives. The Castilian businessmen's opposition to the statute—covered over as it might be with " *Viva España!*"—had an obvious origin. Since Catalonia bore taxes double those of other provinces, there was reason to fear that even limited autonomy for the *Generalitat* would increase taxation elsewhere. Civil servants in the bureaucratic center, Madrid, were anxious lest part of the administrative mechanism be torn from their jurisdiction and housed in another section of the country. Professors of law, such as the eminent Sánchez Román, were deeply distressed by the constitutional definitions of the statute. Spain might conceivably have been a federal state, they reasoned, but since articles of the constitution had decreed that Spain was an "integral state with autonomous regions" the "liberties" of Catalonia were too extensive. José Ortega y Gasset and Miguel Maura in their turn opposed any "pact" with an autonomous region as an infringement of Spain's sovereignty. More rowdyish elements in Madrid, in their boisterous attempts to impede the passage of the statute, resorted to shearing off the locks of a famous Catalan poet.

After a debate which lasted through the torrid summer the *Estatuto* was passed on September 9, 1932, by a vote of 314 to 24. Both Catalan and Castilian were recognized as official languages in the autonomous region; relations between Catalonia and other parts of Spain were to be carried on in Castilian. The *Generalitat* was granted its own parliament, schools, and the control of public services. The central government reserved to itself the right to intervene only when a serious threat to public order warranted the intrusion. Should controversies arise between the *Generalitat* and the central government, the constitution had already designated the Tribunal of Constitutional Guarantees as arbitrator.

The movement for Basque autonomy, which followed the lead of the Catalans, was complicated by the existence of a strong traditionalist party, which opposed the central government on religious issues and demanded a concordat with Rome.[5] Since the Basques had always enjoyed autonomous rights in the determination of their tax levies, ultimate decisions on their status could be delayed. Local privileges, limited though they were, had afforded them the means of building roads superior to those of other provinces and of providing themselves with more extensive educational facilities. Though their statute was first proposed in 1932 it did not receive final ratification by the Cortes until after the outbreak of Franco's rebellion in 1936, when munificent grants from the Republican government helped to solidify Basque loyalty. For a moment the resurrected Basque parliament sat in Bilbao; then it was forced to flee before the projectiles of Junker airplanes. In the early days of May, 1937, the people saw Guernica, the seat of its medieval assemblies, razed to the ground.

Throughout the early years of the Republic's existence similar plans for statutes of autonomy were drawn up to cover other major provinces—Galicia, Valencia, even Andalucía. Nationalist feeling was reborn in sections where it had long seemed dead. On June 28, 1936, only a few weeks before the insurrection, the Galicians conducted a plebiscite on their statute of autonomy; they were so filled with the ardor of local patriotism that they appeared unmindful of the deep crisis of the Republican regime. The meeting of Galicians held in Madrid on June 21, 1936, must have seemed anachronistic to a citizen of one of the great centralized states of modern Europe. The first speaker, a member of a nationalist Galician youth organization, described the persecutions which the Galicians had endured at the hands of the central government:

We are an independent political unit! We have a personality of our own. We have a soul of our own. We demand liberty for Galicia in order to afford all the creative elements in our people free play. We are distinct from all other parts of Spain in our economy, our geography, our social life, our language. We have a form of speech which can better express our souls than any other tongue in the world. This is no artificial creation. It is a biological fact. In an economic sense our industries have always suffered because of favors bestowed upon the industries of other parts of the Iberian peninsula. We have seen our fisheries and our fruit production driven to ruin in order to support other sections of the country. At the same time we have suffered in the partition of tax levies, a disproportionate burden having been thrust upon our shoulders. . . . We have crossed the Atlantic and we have colonized South America, but we have no cities of our own. [On the platform was a banner sent by the Galicians of Gary, Indiana, to their compatriots in Madrid.] . . . Why cannot we too partake of the renaissance which is sweeping over those Baltic countries, Lithuania, Latvia, and Poland. . . . Our souls thirst for freedom!

Galician songs by a chorus of Madrid shop-girls and office clerks were pierced by a peculiar drawn-out yodel which only Galicians can appreciate, and the audience dispersed to cries of "Long Live Galicia!"[6]

Such was the spirit of a revived regional nationalism, which acted as a smoke screen for the most vital economic and social problems convulsing Spain. Not even the unfurling of fascist standards welded all the provinces of the Republic into one national body. Revolutionary Catalonia's comparative indifference to the plight of Madrid during the capital's darkest moments in November, 1936, betrayed the survival of a separatist pipe dream.

The Agrarian Reform

In a country where 16 million of the 24 million inhabitants lived on the land, the condition of agriculture and of those who tilled the soil was naturally the paramount issue, far graver than romantic nationalism. Ever since the eighteenth century Spanish reformers, following in the footsteps of the great Jovellanos, had at regular intervals formulated projects for an overhauling of the agrarian system. Government commissions had conducted superficial inquiries, and a few experimental changes had been hazarded. Actually, the solution of the problem had made little progress by 1931, although the most backward Baltic, Balkan, and Central European states had put through their agrarian reforms shortly after the World War.

The advent of the Republic dramatized the lot of the agricultural worker. When Berenguer, during his short political interlude in 1930–1931, suspended the irrigation works and the road building which Primo de Rivera had begun, thousands of unemployed rural laborers were left as a heritage to the Republic. In 1931 slumping prices in grain and olives further aggravated the agricultural and industrial difficulties. Wine exports fell as the European crisis became more acute and France raised her tariffs. The complete failure of the olive crop threw thousands of laborers out of work. According to estimates of the Communist Party there were in 1931 at least 600,000 unemployed in Spain. Toward the end of 1930 landworkers, tenants, peasants, and small holders had participated in great rural strikes which were sweeping through the South. When Galán led his abortive republican uprising near Huesca on December 12, 1930, a thousand peasants flocked to his standards to join the mutinous soldiers. In view of the ominous potentialities of peasants even in the service of the ideal republic all politicians—conservatives, monarchists, Right Republicans, and Socialists—competed with one another in the forcefulness of their pronouncements about the dire necessity for agrarian reform.

On December 31, 1930, official statistics of the distribution of land were still being compiled. A cadaster for only 27 provinces of Spain covering about 51 per cent of the total surface of the country, mostly in the southern half of the peninsula, had been completed. Ferdinand Kriessmann's analysis of the agrarian problem, based upon this limited though singularly reliable material, is in many ways preferable to the more general estimates of the journalist-critics who have glibly poured forth figures for the whole of the country. While the "conclusions" of this work, *The Spanish Agrarian Problem and Attempts at Its Solution,* reflect the unfortunate political environment of the Third Reich, the statistics themselves and their arrangement retain much of the solidity of another epoch of German scholarship.[7] The accompanying table is a summary of Kriessmann's study.

DISTRIBUTION OF LAND HOLDINGS IN SPAIN

	Number of parcels	Percentage of total number of parcels	Total area covered, hectares	Percentage of total area in cadaster	Average size of parcels, hectares
Parcels under 10 hectares each	10,016,194	98.06	8,014,715	35.81	0.80
Parcels 10 to 100 hectares	169,472	1.66	4,611,789	20.56	27.21
Parcels 100 to 250 hectares	16,305	0.16	2,339,957	10.43	143.51
Parcels over 250 hectares	12,488	0.12	7,468,629	33.20	
Total	10,214,459	100.00	22,435,090	100.00	

South of León and Old Castile the number of small holdings decreased and the *latifundios,* the great estates, became more numerous. The table and its percentages, nevertheless, fail to reveal how truly appalling land monopoly was in Andalucía. Since each holding in the cadaster is computed separately, a landlord's name might appear a number of times in the records of a province, but his land would be considered each time as a distinct parcel.   The properties of his wife would also have a separate and individual entry.   This system of tabulation would, moreover, have greater significance in estimating the number of *latifundios* than the number of middle-sized or small parcels because a peasant was not likely to have tiny plots spread over various sections of a province.   Thus in the whole of the cadaster 1,790,026 proprietors are recorded, of whom 1,774,104 (99.1 per cent) own less than 250 hectares each, or together 11,366,390 hectares, *i.e.*, about one half of the total; some 10,000 families controlled the other half, or 11,068,700 hectares.

While the southern provinces, covered by the cadaster, were the areas of great estates on which laborers (*braceros*) eked out an existence, in the northern provinces—Galicia, Asturias, Navarra, and Aragón—the estates were divided and subdivided into such minute parcels that a single holding rarely yielded enough for subsistence.   Since the latter provinces were not included in the new cadaster, Kriessmann was able to offer only isolated examples of the land distribution, striking enough in themselves; for instance, in the district of Santa María (Galicia) six or seven hectares were divided into some 80 to 120 parcels. In these provinces it was customary to lease and sublease land, sometimes to the fourth degree, the whole structure weighing upon the lowest ranks of the agricultural proletariat.   As a result hordes of Galicians would each year at harvest time take to the road to find temporary employment in the south, while their wives and children cared for their own bits of land.   The wages of these agricultural laborers were often lower than two pesetas a day.

Postwar agitation among the masses had forced the rulers of other agricultural countries in Europe to pass laws of agrarian reform in order to end the preponderance of vast untilled domains. In Spain, to quote further estimates, 31,000,000 out of a total of 50,000,000 hectares belonged to still uncultivated or inade- quately cultivated large estates.   And while these lands lay fallow hundreds of thousands of peasants were forced either to abandon their native soil or to starve.   "Men without land, land without men," was Cristóbal de Castro's pithy description of his country's plight.[8]

In Avila, Salamanca, Ciudad Real, Palencia, Zamora, and Saragossa, there were many seignorial villages (*pueblo de señorio*) where lands, houses, and even the church belonged to a lord, and when rents were not paid the inhabitants could be forced to emigrate. According to custom and law prevailing in these districts, a variety of feudal dues was still levied on the peasants, and any tenant could be driven off his plot if he failed to show due respect to the lord, the lord's relations or his representatives. Cristóbal de Castro laconically reports that in Sobradiel, a village some 16 kilometers from Saragossa, the tenants who had dared to join a League of Peasants were driven *en masse* from the property of their master, the Count of Sobradiel.[9]

Soon after the declaration of the Republic Fernando de los Ríos, then minister of justice, announced that before Michaelmas 70,000 peasants would be settled on the land. On the first anniversary of the new regime the Law of Agrarian Reform had not yet been debated. In the meantime many peasants, awaiting favorable action from the Cortes, stopped paying rent. The landowners, with unknown legislation before them, tried to avoid further investment in planting. Hundreds of estates were put up for sale; land values fell; no one would touch the properties. The delay of the agrarian reform, the uncertainty and wild rumors which this procrastination engendered, wrought more havoc than any drastic measures would have done. In some districts the peasants who had heard reports about proposed expropriations and who saw the *latifundios* lying before them proceeded to institute an agrarian reform by themselves. Early in June, 1932, an incident was reported in the province of Salamanca: 200 peasants, led by their mayor, marched to the estate of the local count and, after much altercation, divided his land among themselves. They then moved on to the office of a government official to register their new properties. Such attempts to accelerate the tempo of the agrarian reform through extralegal methods were usually suppressed, though in isolated instances the peasants were successful and numerous contradictory claims were established. In districts where peasants were on the march, landowners summoned the hated rural patrol of the Civil Guard and blood was spilt.

Marcelino Domingo's Law of Agrarian Reform was finally passed on September 15, 1932, by a vote of 318 to 19. The transformation of the government's original legislative proposal through a number of readings was typical of what occurred with other projects of reform. Its first draft, presented to the Cortes in 1931, still bore a marked revolutionary character. As Fernando de los Ríos had announced, the government proposed to settle 60 to 75,000 families on the land before the end of the year. No Spaniard was to possess more than 300 hectares; there was no reference to compensation for expropriated lands; and a special tax was to pay for the financing of this thoroughgoing agrarian reform. According to the second and more moderate draft, an estate was not to be expropriated merely because its area exceeded a certain limit. The criterion of judgment was to be not the area but its usefulness, i.e., the thoroughness with which the land was being cultivated; untilled areas alone would fall under the government's jurisdiction. Expropriation without indemnity would affect only feudal properties, the royal domain, and the lands of the church and its religious orders. By March, 1932, in the third draft, the very tenor of the original law suffered a change. Only feudal properties would be expropriated without indemnity, while for other lands favorable financial arrangements were provided, including even monetary compensation. Sound conservative opinion, expressed by the London *Times*, was elated by the metamorphoses: "The original land reform scheme . . . has been redrafted three times, and each time some of its more extravagant features have disappeared. The fourth draft just tabled in the Cortes may be further modified in course of debate."

The law of September 15, 1932, established an Institute for Agrarian Reform as the recognized agency for the execution of the measure. Officially, the law applied to the whole of Spain; actually, with the exception of state lands and feudal properties, colonization was to be concentrated in the eight provinces of Andalucía, the two of Extremadura, and the isolated provinces of Ciudad Real, Albacete, Toledo, and Salamanca. The Sanjurjo revolt of August 10, 1932,[10] and the manifest complicity of many groups of nobles in the uprising, conveniently afforded the government an excuse for demanding the confiscation of lands belonging to the grandees of Spain. When the Right protested that this special provision against members of a class (some 300 dukes, marquises, and counts) was a violation of the egalitarian principles of the constitution, the government referred to the clauses about the social function of property which had been transgressed. Indemnification for the seizure of nonfeudal lands was declared on the basis of their taxable value; their owners were to be paid in state bonds the disposal of which was restricted.

Expropriated land became national property, and the newly settled peasants were considered tenants of the government. A variety of methods of allotment was envisaged. Land in the vicinity of large cities could be divided into small holdings, to be farmed by single families. Communities of peasants on large estates were allowed to decide by vote whether they wished to cultivate collectively or individually the lands assigned to them. The government preferred communal groups, and the Institute for Agrarian Reform was empowered to promote cooperatives both for the purchase of materials and for the sale of produce. There was a natural concern among the more provident members of the Republican-Socialist coalition about the political principles which might be espoused in the future by individual peasant proprietors, as well as a sincere dread lest the peasants again fall under the dominance of *caciques*. To disseminate the techniques of the best agronomists and to raise the production level of the ordinary peasant, the law provided for the erection of experimental stations. Finally, the ancient leases and tithes of peasants became subject to revision; if a municipality could prove that certain commons had been acquired illegally by their present proprietors the lands might, upon investigation, be returned to the village.

The Institute for Agrarian Reform was composed of technicians together with an equal number of farm workers, proprietors, and settlers. The choice of workers' delegates was limited almost exclusively to the Socialist General Union of Workers, with the consequence that unorganized farm laborers or those affiliated with the Anarcho-Syndicalist National Confederation of Labor were rarely granted a voice in the deliberations of the Institute. Financial provisions for this pretentious piece of agrarian legislation were patently inadequate. When summing up the costs of their extensive reform program in various branches of social and economic life the ministers talked in terms of 5,000,000,000 pesetas. For the nonce the Institute for Agrarian Reform was endowed with the paltry sum of 50,000,000 pesetas. The extent of the grandees' land which had been made immediately available by the *Sanjurjada* was unknown. More money was necessary, not only for the compensation of landowners, but also for the purchase of new materials and machinery, lest the peasant starve on his own land as he had on the land of his lord.

After the debates in the Cortes had subsided, the technicians of the new Institute for Agrarian Reform went into action. While surveyors and engineers moved laboriously through the provinces of Extremadura, the peasants and the Civil Guards clashed on the borders of large estates. The peasants were impatient. They stole acorns for their pigs and were shot. Nor did they treat their ancient enemies, the Guards, with grace and forbearance. They mocked and openly attacked these stalwarts of the existing order. The lot of a few Civil Guards in their isolated station in the midst of a hostile land-hungry peasantry, often waiting in vain for their grants, was not a happy one.

The Azaña cabinet was too absorbed in the suppression of revolutionary disorders on the Right and on the Left to appease the peasants. The Republic was born to an economic crisis. Before it could put flesh on the legal bones of the Agrarian Reform, mutilated as they were, a reactionary government came into power through the elections of November, 1933. In the eight provinces where the Agrarian Law was to be applied originally there were available 266,453 hectares of land belonging to the former grandees of Spain. Yet the statistical record of the Republic's accomplishment in that area during the first years of its existence was no cause for thanksgiving among the peasantry of Spain. In the volume of the *Anuario Estadístico* appearing on September 18, 1935, it merely was announced that 8,559 laborers had been settled on the land and that collectives (*arrendamientos colectivos*) in 452 communities, comprising 65,771 persons, had been established.[11] "What has the Republic given you to eat?" became the provocative question of the rightist agitators. On Good Friday, 1935, 15,000 peasants of Catalonia, the *Rabassaires*, who shared crops with the owners of their land, marched through the streets of Barcelona beneath banners which repeated a simple age-worn slogan: "The land belongs to those who cultivate it."

The Religious Orders

Crucial as the agrarian problem may have been, the anticlericalism of the Socialist and Republican intellectuals in power remained the most pungent condiment in their whole feast of reforms. Economic issues called for solutions which were often beyond their capacity or design; antagonism toward the church touched their souls. The crusade of the intellectual godless has always had something bitter and spiritual about it. Among Spanish peasants, influenced by revolutionary propaganda, this feeling had more homely expressions: the mayor of a tiny village is said to have telegraphed to the central government: "We have declared for the Republic. What shall we do with the priest?"

In various outbursts of anticlericalism during the nineteenth century the Spanish government had expropriated church lands. After the Restoration of 1874 the Bourbon monarchy proclaimed the indissolubility of the bond which tied it to the church by compensating religious orders for their confiscated properties with threefold grants. When Alfonso XIII was on the verge of abdicating he did not, however, enjoy unflinching support from the clerics who graced his antechambers. Writers of memoirs have reported that ecclesiastics were frequently numbered among the hordes of devoted followers who swarmed in and out of the Model Prison in Madrid when the Revolutionary Committee was holding court. If it is the will of God and the people that Spain should have a Republic again, was the pious thought, then the church would perhaps find ways of accommodating itself to the new system. It might thus hope to escape the vengeance of Republican anticlericalism and the horrors of church burning which had broken out whenever Spain experienced a violent political crisis.

Members of the lower clergy who in 1929 had been paid pittances from a government budget felt no loyalty toward the fallen dictator. The knottier problem was whether the princes of the church, many of them living in ostentatious luxury and indifferent to the physical suffering of their flocks, would alter their natures in time to evade the punishment of the anticlericals. These sinful mortals were often less flexible than the policies of the Mother Church. The new sympathy for Spanish social democracy on the part of some churchmen was therefore rightly regarded with suspicion by the people. Anticlerical excerpts from Rousseau, Volney, and Kropotkin appeared in popular translations and the workers devoured them. After a month of "peaceful revolution," enraged mobs set fire to churches and drove nuns and monks out of their retreats. Socialist ministers with anticlerical traditions announced that they would rather see all the monasteries in Spain leveled to the ground than shed the blood of a single republican.

The church, thus harassed, sought shelter in a "liberal" position. It would suffer in silence a partial disestablishment, even the declaration that Catholicism was no longer the state religion, if only its properties were respected and guarded. Was it not a corporation in public law? The Republican-Socialist coalition under Azaña granted none of the clerical pleas; instead it framed constitutional articles hostile to the religious orders and passed a set of supplementary laws which outraged Catholic conservatives.

The Spanish government armed itself with statistics. The regular clergy, it maintained, numerous as they were in 1900, were on the increase, growing even faster than the population.[12]

GROWTH OF THE SPANISH CLERGY

Year	Number of ecclesiastics	Number of ecclesiastics for every 10,000 inhabitants
1900	54,738	29.42
1910	59,896	30.02
1923	71,815	33.16
1930	81,400	34.54

Some provinces, such as Guipúzcoa, showed figures much higher than the general average. For the years comprised in the census, the proportion of priests for every 10,000 inhabitants in this Basque province varied from 83.28 to 145.44 to 131.43 to 125.39. In 1930 there were 4,908 religious communities in Spain, housing 20,642 male and 60,758 female inmates. The statistical annual of the Spanish government registers the varying purposes to which these institutions were devoted.[13]

CHURCH ESTABLISHMENTS IN SPAIN

Purpose	Number of institutions for	
	male clients	female clients
Education..........................	514	1,432
Charity............................	35	1,128
Contemplation......................	147	863
Other ends.........................	326	463
Total...........................	1,022	3,886

Of all the religious orders the Jesuits had incurred the most profound hatred; hence a decree of January 23, 1932, hastened to dissolve the Society of Jesus in Spain on the constitutional ground that its members were subservient to an alien power. Final judgment against other religious orders was deferred until May 17, 1933, when the ecclesiastical property was declared to be national and the state granted the Catholic church only the use of its buildings for worship. A few rightist deputies in the Cortes alternated obstruction with abstention in a supreme effort to salvage the economic power of the church. Despite their tactics religious orders were prohibited from teaching, and monks and nuns were no longer allowed to run minor industrial establishments in their cloisters. The law further stipulated that all education by religious orders had to cease on October 1, 1933, except for primary schools, which were granted extension until December 31.

In desperation the rightists turned to the country, seeking to provoke a mass protest against this violence to church ownership. It was maintained that the law deprived citizens of the right to work. Liberty for parents to direct the schooling of their children was claimed as another inalienable right. "Freedom of education!" was the slogan. Catholic apologists tried to turn the tables on Azaña by invoking Jacobin phraseology. Anticlericals seldom deigned to reply. When church spokesmen wept and begged for pensions from the state for parish priests over sixty, the anticlericals parried that if the Spanish ecclesiastical hierarchy administered its endowments equitably it would be

able to provide for its own ministers.   Where was the reputed
freedom of religious worship, asked the Catholics, if the church
had to apply to civil authorities of municipalities for permission
to conduct public manifestations of the cult on feast days?
Permission, moreover, was not always obtained when the
officials feared popular counterdemonstrations.   Holy Week in
Seville would lose its quondam splendor.   Republican-Socialist
leaders tersely retorted to clerical attacks by renaming streets
with religious appellatives after proletarian leaders. At the height
of the anticlerical fever the street where stood the Cathedral of
Toledo became the "Calle de Carlos Marx."

Alcalá Zamora, the president of the Republic, who had first
risen to a defense of Catholic privileges during the constitutional
debate in October, 1931, kept the decree prohibiting further
instruction by the religious orders in his pocket for a whole week.
But he ultimately signed it, thus incurring the temporal antagonism of the Left Republicans for his delay and risking eternal
damnation for his final assent.   The Pope, who had hitherto
remained aloof, issued the encyclical *Dilectissima nobis* to his
bishops on June 3, 1933.   In the name of the "civil liberty"
safeguarded in the Spanish constitution he violently protested
the persecution of Catholics.   He first cautioned against political
interference by the church, and then with apparent inconsistency
condemned the separation of church and state as a "very great
error."   When bishops received the Papal word they excom-
municated "those responsible for the passage of the law" and
prohibited Catholic parents from sending their children to state
schools.   Religious war flared forth.[14]   "Save the souls of the
little children!" became a cry of the church militant which could
rouse many an indifferent Catholic.

Secular Education

If the reactionaries succeeded in subordinating the agrarian
reform and the thorny problems of industrial legislation to the
religious issue, the reformist Socialists, threatened with defeat
in the spiritual sphere, could soon be discredited in the temporal.
Therefore the Azaña cabinet, conscious of the vital necessity of
endowing their country with a secular conscience, undertook to
build within a few months a whole new school system intended to
become the spiritual armor of the new Spain.

When in 1919 Walter A. Montgomery, an American investigator, wrote a report on *Educational Conditions in Spain,* he estimated that only about 59.35 per cent of the population could read and write.[15] Teachers' wages, he found, had changed little since 1859. Though a Ministry of Education had been created in 1900 its budget was only an insignificant fraction of what was normally expended on military affairs. After Primo de Rivera improved educational facilities it was recorded in 1928 that 2,292,486 children attended school. The monarchy left the Republic 35,716 institutions; if compulsory education were to become a reality at least 27,000 more schools would be required. Fernando de los Ríos planned to build them at the rate of 7,000 a year for five years, his project being financed by a loan of 400,000,000 pesetas from the state and another 200,000,000 from the municipalities. At first the government hoped to use confiscated Jesuit buildings to house the new schools. But it soon found itself thwarted because inquiry revealed that these properties were usually registered in the name of laymen; thus the state was forced to pay indemnities. The Minister of Education estimated that 350,000 children had been taught in the institutions of the church; *El Debate,* the clerical organ, claimed that 600,000 had been provided for prior to the passage of the decree against the religious orders. Immediate measures were imperative when even agnostics suggested that a bad clerical education was better than none at all and when ecclesiastics were ready to depict a Spain made ignorant by the Republic.

In retrospect, the actual achievements of the new Ministry of Education appear to be among the positive aspects of the whole scheme of reform. In 1931, 7,000 schools were established in accordance with the schedule; in 1932 budgetary handicaps limited the increase to 2,580. Special courses were inaugurated to improve old teachers and to instruct new ones. There was something heroic about raising teachers' salaries at a time when they were being slashed in the richest democracies of the world. Traveling theaters with museums attached were organized to introduce the fruits of modern civilization and culture into isolated hamlets in the hills. In 1932 pedagogic missions, bearing the message of the progressive Republic to the most backward communities, established no less than 1,181 free public libraries in villages to which they often had to journey on donkeys.[16]

An International University was created at Santander in the former king's summer palace, and royal stables were transformed into comfortable classrooms. Attempts were made to reorganize the entire university system, with intent to divert Spanish students from professions like law, which suffered from an overabundance of practitioners, to technical and scientific fields where Spain needed new talent. Universal education, thought Fernando de los Ríos, would make the peasants and the workers and the intellectuals of Spain appreciate the true worth of the Republic.

Unfortunately, in the fall of 1933 when the new laws against teaching by the religious orders were about to become effective, a cabinet crisis caused the Socialists and the more virulent anticlericals to be dropped from the government. For a while thousands of young people had no schools to attend. Then compromises were arranged by one of Lerroux's Radicals who had become minister of education; religious schools were opened under the direction of priests whom superiors allowed to lay aside their cowls. Religious instruction continued and the crucifixes which had been torn off the walls of classrooms in the early days of the Republic were replaced.

Thus most of the reforms of the Republican-Socialist coalition were allowed to pass through their legislative phase in the Cortes only to be sabotaged during the process of execution. The ideals of Azaña and his friends were of the purest—in terms of progressive, anticlerical, mildly Socialist modernism. These leaders were not all dreamy utopians; many of them fancied themselves to be astute realists. Their reforms, however, instead of creating a new soul for Spain only served to reveal further strife and antagonism in the old one. Novel decrees hardened the class consciousness of amorphous groups. Each new law seemed to act like some marvelous chemical turning social fluids into solids. Instead of peace and harmony there was class war. Instead of dominating the scene the Center was devoured.

NOTES

1. *Anuario Estadístico de España, Año* xvii, 1931, pp. 490–492, Madrid, 1933.
2. Manuel Azaña, *Una Política*, pp. 145–146, Madrid, 1932.
3. Julio Milego, *El Problema Catalán*, chaps. ii–iii, Madrid, 1916.

4. See A. Rovira i Virgili, *Catalunya i la República*, Barcelona, 1931; Jaime Aiguader, *Cataluña y la revolución*, Madrid, 1932.
5. José Antonio de Agire y Lebuke, *Entre la libertad y la revolución*, chap. x, Bilbao, 1935.
6. From notes of the author taken at the meeting.
7. Ferdinand Kriessmann, *Das Spanische Agrarproblem und die Versuche zu seiner Lösung*, Stuttgart, 1934.
8. Cristóbal de Castro, *Al servicio de los campesinos*, Madrid, 1931. Text refers to subtitle of the book.
9. *Ibid.*, pp. 140–141.
10. See *infra*, pp. 111 ff.
11. *Anuario Estadístico, Año* xix, 1934, pp. 214–215, Madrid, 1935.
12. *Ibid., Año* xvii, 1931, p. 664.
13. *Ibid.*, p. 667.
14. London *Times*, June 5, 1933.
15. Walter A. Montgomery, *Educational Conditions in Spain*, Washington, 1919.
16. *Anuario Estadístico, Año* xviii, 1932–1933, p. 66, Madrid, 1934.

Chapter VI

AZAÑA'S COALITION

A middle-class Spaniard did not have to succumb to the anti-Republican propaganda of the period, which differentiated between the "vital" country and the country as mirrored in the Cortes, in order to realize that the reactionaries could muster far mightier forces than appeared to be represented by the scattering of agrarians and Basquo-Navarre traditionalists in the assembly. Nobles and their retinues, princes of the church, bankers and merchants who had amassed fortunes through the purchase of concessions from the dictator—these could, with the economic power in their hands, engineer a movement to combat the reforms of the Republic. As the new laws were ground out the reactionary groups had a blunt and straightforward goal: the defense of their privileges, be they feudal holdings and ecclesiastical properties with centuries of "right" behind them, or freshly granted monopolies whose corrupt origins had not yet been covered over with the moss of long possession.

Writers could easily be bought to prove that the new reforms were running counter to the main currents of the Spanish spirit and to scribble about Religion, Fatherland, Nationalism, or the protection of the "true" Spain against the alien doctrines of Marxism. When the pen was inadequate, *pistoleros* (gunmen) could be paid to assassinate Republicans and provoke riots at so much per misdeed. A plea for the preservation of vested interests was dressed up in sacred garments; the "defense of religion" —the outstanding cliché—worked as well among ignorant womenfolk in tiny villages as among elements of the middle class in the cities. The vociferous upholding of the army's prestige, which had suffered under the reign of the clerks, was another traditionalist technique. In all, the reaction was a formidable alliance of moneyed classes relying on agile tongues.

To punish treason to the new state Azaña had at his disposal the Law for the Defense of the Republic—and he used it rather promiscuously. Monarchists were imprisoned without trial and were kept behind bars for years before formal charges were presented.[1] The fate of the Miralles brothers, arrested on May 10, 1931, became the most notorious of these cases. The youths were not treated badly; they were allowed to paint, to write poetry, and even to visit their sick grandmother on one occasion, but they could not enjoy republican freedom. Through June, 1932, the Cortes kept voting on commissions which were to judge those responsible for the dictatorship of Primo de Rivera. Though the punitive measures were eminently justified, the pettiness of the legal paraphernalia outraged the friends of those accused and made pseudo martyrs. The Republican intellectuals taunted their inveterate enemies while these were ready for killing. When monarchists opened clubs and exchanged seditious feelings in secret, the government's officers, as a variant from shutting down syndicalist trade-union halls, would invade the hide-outs of the reactionaries. One day the courts would ring with the revolutionary songs of anarchists and communists, the next, with the traditionalist hymns of monarchists. Forms were not always meticulously observed when royalist newspapers were fined and suspended. Miguel de Unamuno, bearing the tablets of the law, invaded the *Ateneo*, the factory of Republican liberty, and brazenly upheld the thesis that the processes of the Spanish Inquisition, which had granted testimonial rights to its victims, compared favorably with Azaña's judicial methods.

The Sanjurjada

On August 10, 1932, after having endured more than a year of molestation, the hapless nobles revolted in Madrid, and they won over General Sanjurjo, the Lion of the Riff, to lead a supplementary rebellion in Seville. The attempt of a few reactionary army officers in Madrid to seize the post office in the center of the city was a failure. A troop of cavalrymen which had set out from Alcalá de Henares to join the movement deemed it wiser to return to their barracks before they had reached the capital. In Seville, Sanjurjo proclaimed himself Captain General of Andalucía and pronounced a "republican dictatorship," abolishing the existing government for its own sake; the workers responded with a general strike, erected barricades, and fought the rebels in the streets. By the time loyal Civil Guards reached the city, the general had already fled. On the road to Portugal he was overtaken and the uprising turned out a fiasco.

The *Sanjurjada* was a cue for the Republic to adopt more severe measures against the reactionaries, and it emerged somewhat strengthened from the trial. Church burnings and revolutionary agitation were the retort of the workers to this aristocratic coup. They demanded violent reprisals against the ancient enemies and the government was inclined to accede to their wishes, though not before it had allowed the Civil Guards to disperse and to shed the blood of the more militant proletarian demonstrators in the squares of Seville. In a few days Azaña filled the Model Prison in Madrid to capacity with a thousand dukes, generals, and their hirelings. General Sanjurjo himself was tried and sentenced to death, though within a day republican mercy for the famous warrior tempered justice and the decree was commuted to life imprisonment. The estates of the nobles implicated in the rebellion were confiscated, and arrangement was made by Casares Quiroga, the minister of the interior, to ship the incorrigibles, at their own expense, to a camp in Villa Cisneros on the west coast of Africa, the same insalubrious colony to which the syndicalists had been deported after their Llobregat revolt in January. The turmoil of the *Sanjurjada* had brought to the surface evidence of disloyalty in the civil service, the judiciary, the foreign service, and the army. Hence one of those periodic demands for a thorough purge was presented. The cleansing was partially effective; those losing their jobs joined the clandestine army of reaction, adding gall to the mixture.

To say that no generals should have lived to revolt twice against the Republic now appears obvious. Generals Sanjurjo and Goded, condemned traitors, survived to march in the front ranks of a far more skillfully prepared uprising in July, 1936. This was a Republic of men of good will. On August 28, 1932, when the tumult of the *Sanjurjada* had subsided, Marcelino Domingo, the Radical-Socialist Minister of Agriculture, described the highly self-conscious pirouetting which was to follow the revolt: "We have learned from the weakness of Kerensky and Madero . . . we shall take a step towards the left."[2]

After the *Sanjurjada* open espousal of monarchical principles became too dangerous for even the most heroic nobles. They therefore devoutly enveloped themselves in the mantle of the church. In July, 1933, with the appearance upon the scene of Mgr. Goma, the new primate of Spain, the church in a decisive though indirect manner assumed the dominant role in the defense of old Spain. The new archbishop of Toledo carefully avoided an open breach with the government lest he suffer the fate of his tactless predecessor, Cardinal Segura. A separate organization, *Catholic Action*, would provide the faithful with correct policies in this new regime, while the church itself was "confined to its symbols." Gil Robles, a young professor of law, came forth as leader of the secular movement for the protection of the church, to form a center about which could gather heterogeneous economic, social, political, and philosophical interests which had been injured by the Republic. This group became the C.E.D.A., the Spanish Confederation of Rightist Minorities, which from humble origins slowly evolved into a resolute clerical-fascist party. Adequately financed from above it wended its way through brambles of reactionary doctrine to emerge unbruised in the saintly garb of modern Catholic populism.

The Anarchists

When Marcelino Domingo intimated that after the *Sanjurjada* the Republican-Socialist coalition was prepared to take a step toward the left, he was probably aware that the Left had already set out to meet the government—with red and black flags, bombs, and clenched fists.

The anarcho-syndicalists, whose numerical strength cannot be estimated with any pretensions to accuracy because the nature of their activities precluded a poll, could mobilize hundreds of thousands of city workers and peasants. Anarchism was the indigenous modern revolutionary movement of Spain. Syndicalism, a late nineteenth century French importation which advocated the erection of a society based on trade-unions alone, had taken root chiefly in Catalonia. Though both doctrines became identified with each other in action because of their common hostility to the state, during the whole period of the Republic the Anarchist Federation of Iberia (F.A.I.) and the Syndicalist National Confederation of Labor (C.N.T.) remained two distinct organizations. The anarcho-syndicalists could be differentiated from Socialists and Communists primarily on the basis of their hostility to any policy of state centralization, whether the class in power were feudal, bourgeois, or proletarian. In their ideal society each town and each village would become a separate unit of social existence. Money would be abolished. There would be a free interchange of products with no all-powerful state to supervise transactions. All men were naturally good. Once tyrannical masters, freaks of the social order, were wiped off the face of the earth, men would cooperate with each other in perfect harmony.

To the anarchists the Republic signified only a change in the mode of repression. At most it meant greater laxity, the gnawing of Socialist conscience whenever the government had to send armed police against workers and peasants seeking bread, a bit of regret in the Cortes when the casualties were too numerous. The anarcho-syndicalists refused to vote for representatives of this regime. They were unwilling to use either the parliamentary system of the monarchy or the Cortes of the Republic, even to effect social reforms. The truckling and the compromises of a constitutional debate were not for them. Too often had they heard of Socialists who, when raised to office, were transformed into bureaucratic underlings of the reigning powers. The historical preconceptions of Marxism, which posited a feudal system, followed by a bourgeois epoch, then a proletarian dictator-ship, and finally a classless society, were meaningless to the anarchists. Their tenets were a-historical; they were bearers of the spirit of revolt in mankind, not elements in a logic of history. Direct action, revolutionary violence, was their weapon. To them trade-unions were legitimate organizations only when devoted to a revolutionary cause. Once established, trade-unions should direct their energies to preparations for the great day on which the general strike would be declared throughout the land and all production paralyzed. Then bourgeois society would be destroyed at one fell blow. Then the era of liberty would be inaugurated.

Freedom of the individual, whatever its implications, was the cardinal doctrine of anarchist philosophy, sponsored by a long line of eighteenth century *philosophes* republished in popular editions. In Spain Rousseau's *Social Contract* and Volney's *Ruins of Palmyra* exerted their last breath of influence. Bakunin was still father of the movement; excerpts from Sorel's *Reflexions on Violence* were its most philosophic expression; and Kropotkin's

Struggle for Bread its most widely read pamphlet. To the amazement of those who examined the small libraries of anarchist trade-unions, even Nietzsche had his place among the theorists because of his exaltation of the individual.

Anarchist hatred of the Catholic church assumed fantastic forms, for many grievances had been stored up against it. Their anti-Catholicism, though often sacrilegious, was mystical in its own sense, possessing a violence and a fervor which can characterize only an ex-Catholic. When in August, 1936, the anarcho-syndicalist workers of Barcelona invaded monasteries to drive out monks who had transformed their houses of religion into fortresses, the workers refused to touch the food stored away in cellars, even though their own supplies were meager. They broke open wine barrels and poured the contents into the gutters. The food had been contaminated by the monks. The invaders were not thieves; they were not looting storehouses; they were fighting their enemies.

The anarchist spirit of self-sacrifice and the passion of their enmity for existing society exhibited a weird grandeur. Rational arguments about the practical necessities of state organization were drowned out by shouts of "Long live Liberty!" The anarcho-syndicalists were the primordial matter from which a successful revolutionary movement could have been built if there had only been time. As it was their strength spent itself in abortive uprisings. Ramón Sender has caught their spirit and recorded it faithfully in his *Seven Red Sundays*. Their simple pseudoscientific materialism was combined with the most sentimental humanitarian creed, though their avoidance of bourgeois emotional forms was bizarre. In Sender's book a young anarchist consoling the daughter of a fallen comrade announced: "Death does not exist. . . . Death is bourgeois."[3] Rather than allow their cities to fall into the hands of the fascist rebel chieftains, anarchists would prefer to put the torch to their own homes and die amid the flames. The frenzy of their hatred for rulers and the warmth of their love for symbols and abstractions are hardly comprehensible to rationalists.

When socialist trade-unionists called strikes nothing prevented anarcho-syndicalists and communist workers from joining in and carrying away the movement with their more militant policies.[4] Throughout the years 1931–1933 there were inter-

mittent threats of a general rising in Andalucía. Peasants
burned mechanical reapers in the spirit of the early nineteenth
century Luddites who saw in new instruments only a further
means of depriving them of work.   Outworn and newborn ideologies competed with each other for the allegiance of the workers
and the peasants.

A Socialist Dilemma

The official Socialist Party of Spain, affiliated with the Second
International, was in a most ambiguous position during the whole
period of collaboration with the Left Republicans.   The Socialists had entered the cabinet with a larger representation than any
other single party in the Cortes.   They had stood for election
in June, 1931, with the only functioning party machine in the
country.   As the months rolled by they became the special
object of attack from the conservative republicans, Lerroux's
Radicals, because of the conspicuous tinge with which they were
shading the whole regime.   The Socialists, forced to compromise with the moderate Republicans and responsible for the
stringent measures of public order taken against strikers, were
continually in danger of losing the support of their own adherents.
Holding down the Ministries of Labor, Public Works, and Justice,
Socialists were more often in contact with the masses than the
other members of the cabinet.   But when they refused to accede
to all the demands of the workers they were faced with the possibility of anarcho-syndicalist and communist inroads into the
ranks of their membership.   On December 18, 1932, confronted
with a general railway strike, Prieto, unwittingly perhaps, yet
concisely enough, expressed the standard dilemma of a Socialist
in power: "As a Socialist I respect the right to strike, but as
Minister of Public Works responsible for communications in
Spain I must see that services are continued."[5]

To avoid the contradictions of this situation one group in the
Socialist Party was in favor of withdrawing its representatives
from the cabinet and maintaining a purer Socialist attitude.
But on October 12, 1932, this view was overriden at a Party
Congress by a vote of 23,000 to 6,000; it was decided to continue
collaboration with Azaña until the whole legislative structure of
reform was completed.   To placate its more militant members
the Congress then proceeded to demand the disbanding of the

Civil Guard, notorious for its clashes with workers and peasants, and the substitution of a rural Republican Guard. This desire was to receive frequent though rather futile expression a number of times during the ensuing years.

By August, 1933, the experience of the parliamentary period, during which the Socialists had time and again been called upon to uphold Azaña's Republic, began to arouse doubts about the wisdom of a collaborationist policy in the mind of Largo Caballero, the veteran Socialist labor leader. For two years, while in the Ministry of Labor, he had refrained from making official pronouncements on party questions, but now he could no longer restrain himself. In the late summer of 1933 his changed attitude manifested itself in militant speeches on the emancipation of the proletariat. The new spirit was quite different from the tone of his admonitions to the workers during the days when he was creating the boards of arbitration. Though he took exception to Russia's international policies he now voiced his approbation of the Soviet system. Nevertheless, the official Communist Party of the Third International refused to accept the revised outlook of Caballero on good faith. Still unconvinced, they accused him of electoral demagogy, of stealing their thunder. Had he not recently been the member of a government which had suppressed the Communist Party organ, *Mundo Obrero*, for eight months?

Communist Parties

During Azaña's premiership Communist Party headquarters were often raided by government shock troops, and many party members were imprisoned. In 1932 Fernando de los Ríos accused the Soviet Union of fomenting revolutionary strikes by sending the Spanish Communist Party fabulous sums. In counterattack the Spanish Communist Bullejos charged: "The Azaña government is converting itself into a pliable and willing tool in the plans of French imperialism, above all of its bellicose intentions against the Soviet Union."[6] More credible perhaps was the Communist accusation that "the only result of the agrarian reform instituted by the Spanish bourgeoisie has been to create some well paid jobs for officials who are 'studying' this question."[7] This Stalinist party, however, could not monopolize the name "Communist." In Catalonia Joaquín Maurín headed a Peasants and Workers Bloc which considered itself a native Communist faction opposed to the Comintern. Andrés Nin, Leon Trotsky's lieutenant in Barcelona, was the representative in Spain of the discredited Soviet leader's revolutionary principles, usually more successful in their epigrammatic formulation than as guides for action.[8] The conflicting Communist groups, expert in mutual vilification, stunted each other's growth and were not numerically significant. Nevertheless, "Russian agents are active in the peninsula" became the regular point of departure for editorials in the London *Times* on the situation in Spain and Portugal.

Lerroux's Radicals

Since a frontal attack on the part of the anti-Republicans would have been impolitic during the early months of reformist enthusiasm, the reactionaries saw their only hope for the time being in the Radical Party under Lerroux. Anyone who opposed the advanced legislation of the Azaña coalition and yet shunned a direct alliance with the remnants of the feudal monarchy joined this new Center group with its eyes toward the Right. Lerroux, a veteran Republican revolutionary, suddenly awoke with a boundless admiration for the Civil Guard as the last guarantee of order, and overnight transformed himself into the bulwark of the bourgeoisie against Socialism. His first bid for power was a demand, early in 1932, that the Constituent Cortes, having fulfilled its mission, should be dissolved. Lerroux's press agents began to make a savior of the turncoat: "With Lerroux Spain will feel herself revivified. He might be for Spain what Poincaré was for France in 1927."[9] Azaña, with a secure majority, was by no means prepared to submit to a Catholic-conservative alliance before he had rendered the Republic meaningful through the passage of those supplementary laws provided for in the Constitution. Lerroux formed an opposition group to harass the coalition and to trim its progressive legislation, though not always to defeat it on a final vote.

By the middle of July, 1932, the Socialist Party, sufficiently outraged by the manœuvers of Lerroux, denounced him in a manifesto as an enemy of the Republic. Lerroux countered with a threat that unless the Socialists were eliminated from the cabinet, he, in the name of the Republican bourgeoisie, would alter his

benevolent opposition to open hostility.   His bombastic appeals
to the country were cut short by Sanjurjo's rebellion in August,
1932—a coup, which, had it been victorious, would have precluded the necessity for a figurehead of the Right Center.   But
no sooner had the rebels passed through the Republic's courts
when Lerroux resumed his obstructionist tactics.   Prieto had
indulged in rather flamboyant outbursts against the American
Telephone Company concession, intimating that it would be
revoked; thereafter Lerroux kept taunting the Socialist minister
for unfulfilled threats against foreign capitalists.   In February,
1933, the Radicals launched a serious campaign in which Lerroux
revealed himself a past master in all the tricks of parliamentary
manipulation.   A whole week was wasted in the discussion of
200 amendments to one of Prieto's projects which called for the
building of a few miles of new road in Alicante.

During the first months of 1933 Spain's attention was, however,
less concentrated on the gladiatorial debates in the Cortes than
on a fresh movement of revolutionary uprisings now spreading
over the country.   1932 had ended with the discovery of bomb
dumps destined to feed an anarchist revolt.   The hand of the
revolutionaries was forced.   On January 8, 1933, civil strife in
Barcelona brought a declaration of martial law from the government.   Maurín's Workers and Peasants Bloc, the Stalinist
official Communists, the Trotskyists, each with their variant of
the revolutionary slogan, defied the authorities and fought for
their party.   The dead were not counted.

Casas Viejas

No sooner had the last explosives been confiscated when rumors
of another bloody tragedy began to seep into Madrid.[10]   Casas
Viejas was an obscure and ancient village in the province of
Cadiz on the border of the 40,000-acre estate of the Duke of
Medinaçeli, which was about to be confiscated.   Prompt censorship and the lack of an official version of what had occurred in
the town made the horrendous facts of the incident even more
dramatic once they became known.   Anarchists weary of the
postponements of the agrarian reform had clashed with local
officials; Republican shock troops had been summoned to quell
the riot.   After they gained control of the situation, they hunted
down the fleeing peasants, captured them, whipped them, and

practiced the *ley de fugas*—allowing the prisoner to escape, then shooting him in the back.   One anarchist, known as Six Fingers, had entrenched himself in his hut with his daughter Libertaria. The troops set fire to the house and the rebels perished in the flames.

During an early debate on the cruelty with which this uprising had been suppressed Azaña tried to gloss over the incident as presenting no unusual characteristics.   Commissions of investigation were formed and sent down to Casas Viejas to silence the critics, for the opposition had at last found a sledge hammer with which to pound away at the coalition government and make its incompetence resound throughout the land.   Menéndez, the Police Prefect, who on August 10, 1932, had acted so bravely, resigned because it was intimated that orders of severe repression had been transmitted to the shock troops.   Captain Rojas, who had conducted the attack on the spot, was arrested.   When five shock troop captains signed a document testifying that the Police Prefect had ordered them to take no prisoners alive, not even the wounded, Azaña was forced to change his tone and declare that these virtual executions had been illegal.   Menéndez was then arrested for attempting to bribe Captain Rojas into assuming blame for the murders.   While Azaña admitted that his government had issued stringent decrees against the rioters, he refused to accept responsibility for a brutality which had exceeded and indeed violated the government's orders.   After protracted debates in the Chamber, during which the Radical opposition had sought to make political capital out of the incident, Azaña was finally upheld by a vote of confidence.

The agony of the government had, nevertheless, set in. Though Azaña may have purged himself of moral guilt for the murder of peasants in Casas Viejas, political consequences could not be averted.   If the Republican-Socialist coalition was not able to preserve order with a minimum of bloodshed, the illumination and idealism of its reform projects would be no saving grace. Others were eager to displace them and show their skill in governance.   *El Fascio*, a new sheet, appeared on the streets of Madrid.

The Fall of Azaña

On April 23, 1933, municipal elections were held in 2,500 villages to elect a total of 15,000 councilors.   These were necessary because the original election held under monarchist auspices on April 12, 1931, had been nullified by the Political Commission of the Republic. Women voted for the first time. Republican ideology had not penetrated into the backward areas, and the appeal of the elaborate reforming program had thus far had only a limited effect. Nothing had really been altered in the ancient mode of existence of these localities. Urban republicanism could easily be diagnosed as an alien growth which devout Spaniards must extirpate. Propaganda about the antichrist in Madrid was rife; no one dared raise his voice against the *cacique* and the village priest. Consequently, the Radicals and the monarchists won an overwhelming majority of seats on the town councils, while the Socialists found themselves reduced to only 2,000—a swift censure of the hybrid Republican-Socialist coalition. On hearing the news reactionaries jubilantly proclaimed that the defeat in the municipal elections would sound the knell of the Azaña government, as two years previously it had foretold the overthrow of Alfonso XIII.

In May, 1933, the political situation became insupportable. Azaña, with his back against the wall, clung to power; in desperation he offered to limit the work of the existing Cortes to a few more supplementary laws. The Radicals rejected his proposal and again demanded that the Socialists be ousted from the cabinet. The municipal elections had proved, they maintained, that the Cortes no longer represented the country. On June 8 the cabinet crisis became acute. President Alcalá Zamora first summoned Besteiro for advice on a new prime minister; then Lerroux; then the intellectuals—Unamuno, Ortega y Gasset, and Dr. Marañón—as if these worthy gentlemen who had once "pronounced" for the Republic were still its spiritual mentors. Indalecio Prieto and Marcelino Domingo were each afforded an opportunity to form a cabinet, but they failed. The Socialists, with 116 members in the Cortes, refused to participate in a coalition with the Radicals, not even in the name of Republican unity.

Finally, to complete the circle Azaña was recalled to the premiership, whereupon he brought forth a new cabinet with essentially the same ingredients as the old one. Fernando de los Ríos revealed a wondrous versatility when he took his third different cabinet post, the Foreign Office; Fernando de Viñuales, a professor of political economy well-known in banking circles, was given Finance; a new Ministry was created for Industry and Commerce.

Incensed by the resurrection of Azaña, Miguel Maura left the Cortes to organize the country against the new cabinet; Lerroux remained behind to torment it. The Cortes itself was now completely disorganized, having lost its morale. While strikes and riots shook the country its members played farces. No quorum was available for the conduct of ordinary business. The Speaker, Besteiro, at his wit's end stopped salary payments until the deputies would vote on the projects before them. They stayed for the disposition of one bill and then fled. Laws were written in a slovenly manner and passed even before flagrant contradictions in their texts were deleted.

On September 4, 1933, the wobbly cabinet received another reprimand directly from the voters. The Tribunal of Constitutional Guarantees had been created; Álvaro de Albornoz, the former minister of justice, had been chosen its president by the Cortes. When popular balloting took place on the ordinary members of the Court, the ministerial parties won only four places as against six for the Right and four for the Center. What more open rebuke than the election of Juan March as a judge, whom the government was then prosecuting for official corruption! The designation of Calvo Sotelo, Primo de Rivera's Finance Minister, an avowed monarchist then an exile in Paris, as the representative of the Lawyers' Association, forcibly injected a foreign virus into the Republic's blood.

In the midst of this general pandemonium the view was propounded that unless a broad republican coalition were called to conduct the elections in November, the Right might win a crushing victory and endanger the very existence of the regime. Azaña resigned once again. On September 10 Alejandro Lerroux was summoned to form a cabinet without the Socialists. Though his government bore the epithet *Republican Concentration* it was the first violent swing to the Right. Azaña's party, Republican Action, and the Radical-Socialists, were represented by new men; the posts which had aroused most controversy, Labor, War, and Public Works, were held by Lerroux underlings. Martínez Barrio, who in 1931 had resigned from the cabinet along with the Radical chieftain, became minister of the interior, with the task of organizing the new elections for the Cortes.

Progressive social action was at an end. The repeal of the reforms promulgated by the previous cabinet was now in order. If the passage of fresh legislation revoking earlier measures were inopportune, the usual Spanish method of failure to enforce would be equally efficacious. The color of the regime was immediately changed by the appointment of 50 new provincial governors and other high officials. Whereupon the Socialists, stranded on a bough, solemnly announced that the original Republican Alliance of 1930 was broken and that henceforth they would remain true to their own party policies, as well they might.

Cabinet Crises

For a number of weeks Lerroux did not venture to present himself in the Cortes. While biding his time he planned an amnesty for "Rightists" in order to conciliate them. When he finally did appear before the deputies on October 2, 1933, he attempted to rally a majority by appealing to the Republican spirit "as a whole," free of the partisanship which had brought the First Republic to its ruin. He could not, however, refrain from reiterating what he had so often maintained while a member of the opposition: that the Cortes no longer represented the country. This paradoxical plea for support naturally drew forth the most vituperative talents from the Left. Prieto scoffingly inquired how the Prime Minister dared ask support from a Cortes which no longer enjoyed the country's confidence. Azaña followed the Socialist's barrage. Alcalá Zamora came in for his share of the lashing for the part he had played as sponsor of the cabinet of *Republican Concentration*. The final vote of censure occurred amidst scenes of disorder which provided café anecdotes for days. Lerroux resigned and tried to rush out of the Chamber before he had heard the replies of the deputies. Speaker Besteiro forced the Prime Minister to remain. Azaña was in fine fettle, his most acrimonious. The Radicals ran in and out of the chamber as if possessed, dogging the footsteps of their chieftain.

The Socialists had set themselves up independently again. Largo Caballero harangued about the dangers of fascism and threatened the bourgeoisie with the armed resistance of the proletariat. The parliamentary manner in which the German

National Socialists, perhaps with the connivance of the president of the Republic, had first entrenched themselves in power could not escape the Spanish Socialists; the parallel was too obvious. During these months the horror stories of the sufferings of labor leaders and Socialists in German prisons and concentration camps filled the air of the continent.

Alcalá Zamora was once more forced to look for a conservative Republican as prime minister. He called the venerables, Sánchez Román and José Manuel Pedregal (a liberal minister of the early twenties), then the inevitable Dr. Marañón, who, as the London *Times* of October 7, 1933, innocently put it, was summoned with the hope that "his friendship with party leaders, his prestige as a Republican, and his great knowledge of nervous disorders may lead to success." The crisis, which superficially bore all the earmarks of one of Alfonso's ministerial intrigues, was far graver; both the General Union of Workers and the National Confederation of Labor were preparing for a general strike. At last a compromise was reached on Diego Martínez Barrio, then considered the right-hand man of Lerroux. The renegade revolutionary himself was dropped; for the rest, essentially the same cabinet was reshuffled. Then, in spite of the demand of the Socialists, Independent Radical-Socialists, and Federalists that Barrio be forced to meet the Cortes, President Zamora granted the new premier the much-sought decree of dissolution. It was Barrio's duty to arrange the elections for November 19, 1933, and he needed ample time to prepare them. His task had, to be sure, been lightened by the opportune appointment of hundreds of Radical administrative officials, whom Lerroux had placed with great haste; for these pawns, so vital in "making" an election, came with a whole bag of electoral tricks, decades old, but still effective in the backward regions of Spain.

The November Elections, 1933

The election campaign was bitter. Azaña tried in vain to organize a bloc on the Left. Gil Robles, the former agrarian, now leader of Popular Action, achieved a greater measure of success in forming a Rightist coalition, which presented a list of candidates covering the whole field, including even Luca de

Tena, avowed monarchist and owner of the much-censored *A.B.C.*, and Calvo Sotelo, the former Finance Minister under the dictatorship. The common program of the Right demanded a revision of the anticlerical and "socialist" legislation of the last Cortes, reform of the constitution, defense of private property, and amnesty for Rightist prisoners. Popular Action, its chest well-filled with church moneys, printed millions of posters for the Right coalition.

Luis Araquistáin, a Socialist who had been ambassador in Berlin, returned to support his party. His speeches at party assemblies in the Madrid *Casa del Pueblo* (House of the People) revealed that he had learned many lessons during his 1933 sojourn in Germany. He advised the Socialists to make use of the polls, though he refused to exclude more violent measures of action from consideration. A group of Socialists was formed for whom the Marxian phraseology of class war and the dictatorship of the proletariat had a new meaning. Should they be elected to power they were determined to hold it, even through force. They would not be pushed from office as blithely as the German Socialist Severing had been in Prussia. Their Republican-Socialist coalition, 1931–1933, had disintegrated. The Revolution was now in order.

As if to counterbalance the Socialist militants, a fascist party appeared under José Antonio Primo de Rivera, a son of the former dictator. He was an orator, well-nurtured on the images and phrases of the German National Socialists. His calls for the fulfillment of Spanish destiny were mingled with a demand for armed vigilance against the Marxists. He scoffed at all programs for his was not a mere political party; it was a union of Spanish patriots. Though he was standing as a candidate for Cadiz, he heaped scorn upon the parliamentary system and urged those who would follow him to prepare themselves with pistols. No sooner had his Spanish Phalanx appeared upon the scene than the number of assassinations increased. These cowardly assaults did not for the most part occur during armed clashes between opposing factions; an isolated working-class leader would drop while on his job.

The anarchists of Barcelona gathered thousands of workers into meetings during which the "guides" of the movement (leaders were not recognized) ordered their followers to abstain from the polls of the reactionary Republic. They anticipated a monarchist victory. If the Leftist Republicans should be goaded into initiating a rebellion, the anarchists planned to join, then assume control, and transform the movement into the "true" Revolution. The working-class parties, though collectively hostile to the Left Republicans, were disastrously divided among themselves. On the very eve of the elections Barcelona was tense with the published details of a supposed anarchist plot to assassinate members of the Catalan Left and Maurín's Communist Workers and Peasants Bloc. Fascist provocators intermingled to complicate further the brew.

Women, whose influence had already made itself felt in the municipal elections, were for the first time voting for members of the Cortes. The number of illiterates in the land was still high, 70 per cent in some districts. Church propaganda was probably the most successful. The clerical minions of secular reactionaries could dramatize the issue as atheist and materialist socialism versus the true faith; thus did monarchists, fascists, and sundry reactionaries crawl beneath the cloak of the bishops. During the elections processions of women marched from the church directly to the polling booths. By special episcopal dispensation nuns who had never left their convents (in accordance with the laws of their order) were allowed to go into the cities to vote. Lerroux and Barrio could normally expect a goodly number of seats for having troubled with the preparation of the elections. In addition, where Rightist candidates could not possibly be placed, the united reactionaries voted for Lerroux's Radicals in return for a benevolent supervision of electoral procedure in other districts. The nonsocialist Left Republicans were isolated, forced to bear the odium of repressive measures of public order and to defend semisocialist policies. Indeed, the Azaña-Domingo group was a forlorn remnant of the coalition of 1931, great slices having fallen to the Right and to the Left.

Many elections had to be repeated when no party won a majority on the first ballot; the elaborate provisions for a vastly complex system of proportional representation delayed the counting; bad means of communication and illiterate election caretakers further muddled the proceedings. It was therefore not until the first week in December that the full blast of the Rightist victory struck the country. The grouping of the

21 odd parties emerging from the glass urns of the Republic is indicated in the accompanying tabulation.

ELECTION RETURNS—NOVEMBER, 1933

Right		Center		Left	
Agrarians	86	Radicals	104	Socialists	58
Acción Popular	62	Catalan *Lliga*	25	Catalan	
Traditionalists and		Conservative Republic-		Esquerra	19
Monarchists	43	ans	18	Galicians	6
Basque Nationalists	14	Liberal Democrats	9	*Acción*	
Indeterminate	2	Independent Democrats	8	*Republicana*	5
		Progressives	3	Independent	
				Radical-	
				Socialists	4
				Catalan Soci-	
				alist Union	3
				Federalists	2
				Radical Soci-	
				alist	1
				Communist	1
Total	207		167		99

The Conservative Republicans and the Catalan *Lliga* were Rightist enough in their outlook to color the Cortes even more deeply than the figures indicate. Later studies of the election of November, 1933, revealed the extent to which the corrupt practices of the local *caciques*, having reorganized their little political kingdoms, had been crucial. Workers had voted for the *cacique's* candidate on threat of being replaced at their jobs by men from adjacent districts; the law restricting the importation of laborers from outside municipalities had not been put into effect with enough regularity to placate the fears of local people. In the outlying districts the Leftist parties could not afford notaries and literate election supervisors; hence many of their votes were not registered. Groups hostile to the Rightist *cacique* were openly intimidated and kept away from the booths. The traditional *pucherazo*—the Spanish equivalent for stuffing the ballot box—was revived with modern ameliorations. Yet in spite of the manipulations of the *caciques*—and in contrast with the distortions caused by the Spanish brand of proportional representation—the combined popular vote of the Right and of the Center did not amount to more than 4,000,000 out of the total ballot of 8,000,000. The Socialist poll of 1,722,000 still represented the strongest single party support. Though the cabinet coalition of Azaña had fallen, Leftist sentiment lived on. Election frauds and the abstention of the anarcho-syndicalists discounted, the country had spoken.

NOTES

1. See Anonymous, *The Spanish Republic,* chap. v, "Suppression of Constitutional Guarantees," London, 1933, for a reactionary's protest.
2. London *Times,* Aug. 28, 1932.
3. Ramón Sender, *Seven Red Sundays,* p. 58, London, 1936.
4. The success of strikes, significant enough to be included in the *Anuario Estadístico,* varied from year to year.

Year	Number of strikes	Number of strikers	Strikes won	Strikes lost
1930	368	247,460	62	106
1931	610	236,177	161	79
1932	435	269,104	97	112
1933	1,046	843,303	416	229

5. London *Times,* December 18, 1932.
6. *International Press Correspondence,* June 2, 1932, vol. XII, p. 479.
7. *Ibid.,* Jan. 12, 1933, vol. XIII, p. 29.
8. See Leon Trotsky's pamphlets, *The Revolution in Spain* and *The Spanish Revolution in Danger,* New York, 1931.
9. José María Carretero, *Lo que no quiere España,* p. 18, Madrid, 1932.
10. George Young, *The New Spain,* pp. 147–148, London, 1933.

Chapter VII

BLACK MASS FOR THE REPUBLIC

In December, 1933, with the apparent consent of the people, the "democratic Republic of workers of every category" fell into the hands of men who, from the first days of their guardianship, were intent upon defiling it. The history of the second Cortes of the Republic may be roughly divided into two periods: during the first year—until the outbreak of the revolution in the Asturias in October, 1934—the odor of political backroom intrigues predominated; during the second year, the smell of blood. While the biennium 1931–1933, for all the weakness of the Republican-Socialist coalition, had been dominated by a few personalities of stature, the dismal interlude from November, 1933, until the elections of February, 1936, is characterized by the jerky movements of fops and puppets.

Alejandro Lerroux, former republican revolutionary, was the self-conscious Mephistopheles who lorded over this witches' Sabbath. He was the prince of phrasemongers. His ideal, he said, was "to govern without the Socialists, but socialistically." His arsenal of thinly veiled tautologies could be drawn upon for every occasion. "The problems in the social order which appear formidable to us require only an economic understanding, the organization of production, and the distribution of riches which result from human labor."[1] By the master's side were ranged the ministerial nonentities, outwitting one another, using their offices as gambling dens, buying and selling permits and concessions. New cabinet formations were frequent, the brevity of their tenure in office rivaling the overnight ministries of Alfonso XIII. The Radicals had won an election, and it seemed as if every prominent party member was to be allowed to disport himself for a while in a ministerial office. A new cabinet meant a reshuffling of the minor bureaucrats, and the Radicals were blessed with many friends. They resurrected that type of official of the monarchy who had performed his tasks

129

so inconspicuously that he was never to be seen in an administrative bureau.

After the elections of November, 1933, the victorious parties had to redefine their tasks. The anomalies of a Republican-Socialist coalition were superseded by the internal contradictions between the Right and the Center. Just as during the first biennium debates had waxed fervent about the tempo of reform, in the second, controversy was waged over the pace and character of the reaction. Which republican limb should be mutilated first? Various cliques on the Right and in the Center sometimes bloated themselves into distinct political formations; then, during an attack from the Left, they would instinctively coalesce, losing their individual identities beneath the common standards of an army of repression. But once the Leftists were routed the struggles within the reactionary parties revealed themselves again.

A Centrist Delusion

From the autumn of 1933 to the October uprising of 1934 three Radical leaders successively headed cabinets of what was known as the Center. The first, Martínez Barrio, engineered the election; Alejandro Lerroux entered in triumph and stayed until April 25, 1934; then he made way for Ricardo Samper, who lasted until October 1. At no point did the Radical Center feel itself well seated, because it was so piteously dependent on the tolerance of the Rightists. A wily one like Lerroux knew that he was only warming chairs for the coming of the monks and the landowners. Others like Alcalá Zamora imagined that the Radical Center in power could lay the foundations for a conservative Spanish Republic. The party of the *juste milieu*, Zamora thought, would bestow upon the land those fruits which can be gathered only upon the middle road, between revolution and reaction. No doubt, the president actually believed in his own castle in Spain. He was antisocialist, but he also distrusted the Rightists like Gil Robles, in spite of their solemn republican oaths.

Though no one felt the necessity for a recasting of the socialistic constitution more than the president, he hesitated to call upon Rightists whose plans for a revision would entrain an overthrow of the whole regime. He remembered that many of them in their former incarnation as Agrarians had even refrained from voting on the constitution. Would it not be illegal for a constitutional lawyer in the highest office in the land now to summon these suspect Republicans and to commit to them the sacred instrument? Zamora was a Catholic and he had taken an oath of office. While he believed in freedom for the religious orders, his faith in certain aspects of the church disestablishment policy denounced by Gil Robles was not shaken. Zamora was Polonius enthroned, gone mad because of the dilemmas confronting him, and seeming to act like Hamlet. Only when powder-filled air from the Asturias was wafted into the presidential palace did he return to his senses. The uprising of the Asturian miners taught him to abandon his constitutional scruples and to follow blindly the men of order. And yet he had to be true to himself; he could not summon Gil Robles to form a cabinet.

Gil Robles—Master of the C.E.D.A.

The policy of Gil Robles, the secular representative of the church, was never allowed to crystallize. The clergy avoided the blunder of entangling itself inextricably in a monarchist alliance as soon as the electorate seemed to be turning toward the Right. Alfonso XIII's exploits in exile, his family troubles, his heirs and their hemophilia stifled monarchist sentiments in the breasts of even the most religious Spaniards. On the continent Catholicism had been experimenting with a new type of government which would comfortably fit a situation in which the temporal lord had been dismissed and no powerful fascist movement, with its two-edged sword, existed. In Austria the church with the aid of devout laymen was slowly eliminating socialism. A clerical-fascist regime did not require the fanfare of a Mussolini or a Hitler, for the church, with centuries of prestige behind it, was not dependent upon the blatant methods of young parvenus. In the beginning it humbly begged to be allowed to exist without molestation, certain that its own subtlety would lead it into the highest council chambers of the state; but in order to survive in revolutionary Spain it was forced to assume the task of leadership, whatever the dangers of reprisal might be, and to modernize its methods. The policy of the German Centrist Party had been a failure because of its listlessness.

Dollfuss was more worthy of emulation, and Gil Robles would act in conformity with the Austrian pattern of Catholic government.

To the church the dynastic problem was far less significant than the confessional one, since it could have hoped for little from a discredited monarchy or a decadent nobility. In its propaganda the church could appeal to the masses with excerpts from the fine passages of scholastic philosophers or the bulls of Leo XIII which preached social justice. The church had never been bound to conceptions of economic *laissez-faire*, and the ideal of the guild and the brotherhood of artisans could be clouded with incense. Memories of the romantic medieval Catholicism of the nineteenth century could be tapped. Instead of aligning itself with crude reaction it could allow some of its members to rant against capitalism and demand an agrarian reform. Gil Robles, with a professional lawyer's discretion, disengaged the church from outworn notions of property:

At this moment two diametrically opposed concepts of property are struggling for supremacy: (*a*) The Individualistic Principle according to which property entails an unlimited right of use and enjoyment which the State must defend. It considers labour a mere merchandise to be regulated by the law of supply and demand. (*b*) Opposed to this egotistic and unrestricted concept of ownership and labour, arises the Socialist State. . . . We defend that concept of property which declares that it is not an absolute right but a right limited by obligations of justice, of charity, of Christian solidarity; that labour is not merchandise but a cooperating element in the work of production and that we must bring about a true harmony of social classes by an intelligent intervention of justice.[2]

Gil Robles was artful enough not to seek power too boisterously or too soon after the electoral victory. Jesuitical ambiguities comprised his book of sacred tactics. "To obtain our end there are two possible courses: the *coup d'état*, which could be the quicker and the more radical; and that which we stand for, the slower but more orderly combat within the bounds of legality. The first I do not reject, but I regard it as the solution only in the case of extreme necessity, a position in which, fortunately, we do not find ourselves."[3] The Radicals had participated in writing the laws of the first biennium, now let them trouble themselves with the details of their repeal! When living costs

were mounting and the peseta was declining in spite of the energetic efforts of the Stabilization Commission, officeholding was a
boomerang. Therefore Gil Robles used Lerroux and his Radicals
for a transition between the sacrilegious Leftist coalition of
Azaña and the new sacred corporative state, rather vague in
form, which the Rightists were planning for Spain. Under
Radical cabinets the educational system was restored to
the religious orders; the Catholic festivals were recognized; the
agrarian laws were rendered ineffective; the pretensions of the
workers were silenced; and the old worthies of the aristocratic
clubs were revered once more. The tone of the regime became
sanctimonious even while the socialistic laws remained on the
statute books. Ground was laid for a concordat with Rome,
for restrictions on the autonomy of the provinces, and for constitutional modifications which would turn the Republic into a
bawd.[4]

The artful juggling of Gil Robles and Lerroux was not so
easy as the two master minds had calculated, for neither was an
absolute chieftain within his own clan. Lerroux had earned
some repute for his speeches before the League of Nations,
delivered from a tribune where seasoned platitudes were better
appreciated than anywhere else in the world. Among his
own followers there was a group, Martínez Barrio among them,
who were laden with doctrinaire objections to the bargain which
had been struck with Gil Robles. In their fashion these Radicals
really believed in the Republic. While Gil Robles was winning
international fame as the strong man of Spain—the final sedative
for that wild people—other Rightists were impatient with the
Popular Action's slow meandering into power. Monarchists
had paid for the C.E.D.A.'s election campaign; now they had
ample reason to fear that the invidious clerics were going to leave
their beloved king in exile. Calvo Sotelo, the monarchist leader,
had bitter words for Gil Robles' treacherous policy. Opinions
which the monarchists gathered from cardinals in the papal
antechambers confirmed the suspicions of loyal supporters of
the Bourbon. "You should not think of a return of the Monarchy," they were told, "but only of transforming this Republic
into a conservative Republic. This is what the Holy See
desires, and the advice which Cardinal Vidal y Barraquer and
Don Ángel Herrera have repeatedly given here."

It was not vouchsafed to Gil Robles to enjoy for more than a year the enviable position of the hawk-eyed censor without responsibility. In the early days of October, 1934, the C.E.D.A. was driven to demand entrance into ministerial office, and the Radicals were forced to admit three outstanding reactionaries into a reorganized cabinet. Don Manuel Jiménez Fernández of the Popular Agrarians, entrenched in the Ministry of Agriculture in order to end doubts about the future of the agrarian reform, Aizpún to arrange matters with the papacy, and Anguero de Sojo in the Labor Ministry were a trio which granted the C.E.D.A. a stranglehold on the new Radical cabinet of Lerroux. The die was cast. When Alcalá Zamora sanctioned this grouping, he opened the way for the reconstitution of the old regime. Machinations would now be followed by overt action.

The C.E.D.A. had always been far more successful in political maneuvering than in the organization of para-military youth meetings. Its leaders would have rejected the epithet "fascist" in a tone of outraged innocence. But in 1933 Gil Robles had taken a trip to Austria to observe Dollfuss's techniques for the winning of the masses, and on his return journey he stopped off to attend the Nuremburg Congress of the Nazis in September, 1933. The working classes under whose very eyes Gil Robles' demonstrations were arranged in 1934 soon became aware of the further implications of clerical fascism. Was the Spanish proletariat to await the fate of the Austrian workers who in February of that year had been bombed in the Karl-Marx-Haus in Vienna by the "peace-loving" Dollfuss? Gil Robles was, they knew, a more brutal Spanish puppet of the Vatican than was the Austrian. Conscious of the legal manner in which Mussolini, Hitler, and Dollfuss had first seized the reins of office, the Spanish workers were determined to forestall a repetition of the tragic play in their own land.[5] A French fascist attempt nipped in the bud on February 6, 1934, encouraged them. Elementary tactics demanded that the workers sally forth against the reaction before it struck the decisive blow.[6]

The October Uprising, 1934

The subsequent October uprising was one of those mass movements which, analyzed by itself as a separate phenomenon, may appear to be a futile demonstration of the revolutionary spirit because of the overwhelming array of forces against it. Just such abortive uprisings, however, give birth to symbols, slogans, tales of heroism and martyrdom—vital for a prolonged revolutionary struggle. A judicious observer, weighing the possibilities of a successful attack on the government at this time, might have realized that most of the necessary elements of a revolutionary situation were absent. Yet despite the defeat, the blood of the Asturian miners nourished the soil from which sprang the victory of the People's Front in February, 1936. The class struggle was accentuated, for now there were thousands of fresh victims to be avenged, whose fate was more graphic than the abstractions of the intellectuals about age-long oppression. Tales of the atrocities perpetrated by the Civil Guards and the army slowly spread throughout the country and leavened the movement. Moors, the ancient enemies of Spain, had been imported from Africa to slaughter the Asturian miners. *U.H.P.* (United Proletarian Brothers) became a rallying cry throughout the land. As crowds shouted these three letters in unison the voice of the people seemed to drown the petty squabbles of labor leaders and Socialist Party stewards. Luis Araquistáin, in an article of extraordinary candor written for *Foreign Affairs* shortly after the October insurrection, has testified to the uncontrollable surge of the uprising:

Most of the older leaders either separated from the movement or were carried in the wake of the younger men, without much hope or determination. . . . When all the details of this extensive and profound revolution can be known it will be found that the younger workers, and they alone, launched it, even against the wishes of the trade-union leaders. It was an irresistible movement, starting at the bottom, with the masses, who were not prepared to accept Fascism without a struggle. The revolutionary tension had reached such a point that, if there had been no explosion, the Socialist proletariat would have broken through its trade-union framework and become incorporated with the Communists and the Anarcho-Syndicalists.[7]

Neither a catastrophic economic situation nor a unified proletariat invited the outburst. In October, 1934, the living standard of the workers was not markedly below what it had been at any time during previous years. The paltry wage gains of the first republican biennium had not all been lost. The strike movement of the agricultural laborers and the city proletariat was poorly coordinated. Peasants suffering from reaction had spent their strength in a premature strike movement in June, 1934. There was general uneasiness in urban centers, but the middle classes were in no revolutionary temper. Though state power was none too firmly organized, the Lerroux-Gil Robles combination had a strong defensive position. If these so-called "objective" conditions were not favorable for a revolutionary crisis, the internal cohesion of working-class organizations did not extend any greater promise. The Workers' Alliances, those attempts at a unity which was to transcend Socialist, Communist, and Anarcho-Syndicalist party lines, were realities only in the Asturias. In other sections of the country the bewildered workers and peasants were fed long editorials of mutual recrimination by rival party leaders.[8]

There were three primary revolutionary centers for the insurrection: Madrid, Barcelona, and the Asturias.[9] Lines of coordination between these localities were pathetically inadequate. The objectives of the movement were never agreed upon by the leaders of the various participating groups; even the few plans which had been formulated were not efficiently carried into the field. The absence of unified strategy made the revolt an agglomeration of individual acts of heroism and individual cowardly defections. It is still far from clear whether the Socialist leadership in Madrid meant the movement to be merely a general strike which would intimidate the government into abandoning the reactionary C.E.D.A., or a revolutionary uprising of the proletariat to seize the state. Divisions within the Socialist Party and the existence of two opposing wings make any definition of intent even less meaningful.

While Largo Caballero stayed in Madrid to direct the movement, Indalecio Prieto, already at odds with his former ministerial colleague, went north to his own haunts in Bilbao, where he is said to have engineered the clandestine unloading of arms from the *Turquesa*. Belarmino Tomás, a friend of Prieto's, led the Socialist military organization in the Asturias. From the outlying provinces accusations of intentional failure to cooperate were soon leveled against the sponsors in Madrid. At the same time attempts to integrate the action of the Anarchists with that of the Socialists and Communists were futile. The former, fearful of Caballero's dictatorship, refused to plan a battle together with the Socialists, even though on the morrow they all were destined to perish on the same barricades. Catalonia, with a predominant interest in preserving its regional autonomy from any reactionary legislation, offered a distinctive and almost alien complex of issues to the proletarian uprising.

The Lerroux group in power could prate "constitutionality" as it imported battalions of Moors from North Africa; it could pose as the defender of a virginal democracy confronted and outraged by an unprovoked revolutionary uprising. What if the C.E.D.A. had vowed to destroy the agrarian reform of the Republic and to restore the church to its former omnipotence? This could not be considered extralegal as long as it was arranged in the Cortes. Mass executions and imprisonments, as an accompaniment of the reactionary legislative program, only lent it vigor. The Spanish Cortes could well imitate the forms of Hitler's Reichstag, where a semblance of legality had always been retained. Even in Spain the reactionaries had learned that the language of legality, because of the comforting and soothing images it conjures up, must never be abandoned, whether or not they are about to precipitate the most barbaric holocausts.

Fiasco—Madrid and Barcelona

On October 8 the Socialist militia in Madrid initiated a guerilla of minor proportions. But though in the Spanish capital there were no large tenement buildings "conducive to class segregation," an easy target for government artillery, the sporadic fighting soon died down. The next day events in Spain were overshadowed by the assassination in Marseilles of the King of Jugoslavia and the French Foreign Minister, Barthou; so Lerroux could make a clean sweep of revolutionary elements without attracting international notice.

In Catalonia the Left Republican leaders in office were so overwhelmed by the task of choosing between alternative courses of action that they ordered their troops to remain inactive while the Madrid government attacked them, though the rights of provincial autonomy were at stake. The representatives of the Workers' Alliances vainly besieged the chiefs of the *Generalitat* with proposals for a united command. *Humanitat*, Catalonia's official voice, had proclaimed the admission of the C.E.D.A.

into the government as an act of treason, but what was to be done? When Companys, the president of Catalonia, continued to tergiversate the Workers' Alliances allowed a threatening note to creep into their pleas for harmony. Instead of seizing the military power, however, the middle-class representatives sat in council hoping that the commander of the Madrid troops, General Batet, would remember the Catalan blood which flowed in his veins. Even when Companys finally proclaimed the Independent Republic in Barcelona and the populace below sang their battle hymn *The Reapers*, he remained tense in the presence of the anarcho-syndicalists. In a defense of his actions which he later presented before a reactionary tribunal there may have been more truth than evasion. Protesting his innocence of treasonable intent he told the court that he had pronounced for the Republic of Catalonia in order that moderate men might remain in control lest violent elements initiate a movement in their own right without the tempering influence of Companys and his Minister of the Interior, Dencás. The persistent refusal of the *Generalitat* officials to arm the people and the sallies of the Catalan police against the rioting anarchists substantiated the contention.

How profoundly shocked the Catalan Left Republican ministers must have been when General Batet advanced on the government buildings after having given intimations of neutrality! The Barcelona radio announcer was in the midst of proclaiming a Catalan victory when his speech was cut short by an agonized death shriek. Catalan troops under the *Generalitat's* command outnumbered Batet's troops; the workers of Barcelona though only equipped with primitive clubs and antiquated "Star" pistols might well have put up a valiant struggle. But Companys the mystic loathed bloodshed. He surrendered and left the Asturians in another corner of Spain to their fate. Azaña, who was conveniently enough in Barcelona at the time, counseled against the whole movement as madness.

Repression in the Asturias

Abandoned by Madrid and Barcelona the workers of the Asturias held out for more than two weeks, munitions factories supplying muskets and hand grenades with which to defy the

Civil Guards. Local republics were proclaimed in the misty mining towns of Mieres and Sama, and revolutionary committees were installed in office. Money was abolished and paper chits substituted. The perfect system of anarchism, with chance communist emendations, had at last been established. Such flashes of the ideal future as were afforded the miners who had risen from the bowels of the earth to fight for liberty were soon blotted out by the bombs of the official army and navy. The struggle for the capital of the province Oviedo was fierce. The workers did not have enough riflemen. Hence in their front ranks the dynamitards would advance, their waists bound round and round with yards of match cord, in their hands bundles of sticks of dynamite, in their mouths freshly lit cigars with which to ignite fuses. Such cannon and rifles as did fall into the hands of the workers were badly manned; no trained army leaders presented themselves. Wild-eyed Moors from Moroccan garrisons were despatched to the hills about Oviedo to hunt down the miners. Sons of Mohammed who, at the height of Musulman conquest in the eighth century, had never been able to subdue the inhabitants of this mountainous province were now ordered into the Asturias as the agents of Christian civilization.

Battleships in the harbor of Gijón shelled the cities; the troops of Generals Bosch and López Ochoa finally subjugated the poorly equipped rebels. When bands of miners were captured they were subjected to such refinements of cruelty that months later their bodies still bore the marks inflicted by the instruments of torture.[10] Simple Oviedo workers have described to the author the punishment meted out to them in the cellars of an old monastery in the center of the city. While they were being whipped their shrieks were accompanied by the monotonous squeaking of a gramophone which played popular tunes for the entertainment of the Civil Guards; above them in the chapel the monks, oblivious to the sufferings of the flesh, intoned a *Te Deum;* in the distance the booming of the cannon re-echoed. . . . One group of miners, which clung desperately to a position long after the defeat of their fellows, was confronted by the spectacle of a barricade of men, arms behind their backs, advancing toward them. The prisoners who formed this living wall suddenly shouted: "Shoot, comrades, the fascists are behind us!" Figures such as Aida Lafuente, a young woman killed defending a barricade, became legendary characters within a few months of their death.

After two weeks of fighting the Asturian workers began to hear the broadcasts of football matches from Madrid; for days they had disbelieved the official announcer who proclaimed the end of the revolt; now they lost faith. The general strike in other parts of the country had not been carried through with enthusiasm. The Asturians had become isolated in their hills while the rest of Spain submitted to the reaction without a pitched battle. To end the bloodshed Belarmino Tomás, head of the Socialist militia, formally surrendered to General López Ochoa and the government troops marched into the battered city of Oviedo in triumph. Tomás, however, could speak only for his own party. The anarchists, fired by a fury and a passion which could not recognize treaties, fought on for days after the official surrender.

On October 14 Largo Caballero was arrested. Prieto fled to France. Communist leaders who contrived to escape sought refuge in Soviet Russia. Newspaper reporters were not allowed to penetrate into the Asturias. Luis Sirval, a Madrid journalist who violated the order, was captured, then shot by his keepers without trial. The presence of the Moors in the northern provinces was never mentioned in the press, while the bloody progress of the Civil Guards was covered by a laconic: "The situation in the Asturias is improving." Throughout Spain municipal councils which included Socialists were dissolved; trade-union halls were closed. The Cortes, meeting in special session, restored the death penalty, and sentences began to fall. When the roll-call disclosed that Socialists and Left Republicans were not in their seats, government spokesmen cynically regretted their absence. Autonomous rights were withdrawn from Catalonia and military rule was established there to deal with restive elements.

When tales of the reactionary reprisals began to seep into Europe, working-class leaders, though they had grown accustomed in 1933 and in 1934 to lacerations inflicted by the mailed fist, were moved to take common counsel. On October 18, 1934, Cachin and Thorez, representing the Third International, met at Brussels with Vandervelde and Adler of the Second. Largo

Caballero was a member of the Executive of the Socialist International; hundreds of Communists had been imprisoned with him. Could not the two outstanding rivals for the allegiance of the world proletariat agree upon a common course of action? The meeting was not fruitful. "We regret that we cannot take immediate action on behalf of Spain," was the Socialist conclusion.

The official news agencies of the world were fed stories about priests whom the workers had burned alive, Civil Guards whom they had dynamited individually, and nuns whom they had assaulted; Lerroux and Gil Robles were depicted as the most recent saviors of Western civilization. Only in January, 1935, when the strict censorship was lifted, did the journalists appear in Oviedo, each with his characteristic apperception. The gentleman from the London *Times* arrived on New Year's Day to survey and evaluate the artistic loss which had been caused by the bombardment. He found the basilica of Santullano (built in 823) intact, noted the hammer and sickle painted on the pilasters and stains of deeper red on the stone pavements. In other churches which had not fared so well, he bewailed each dynamited apostle and waxed eloquent over the former beauty of naves and cloisters which had been destroyed by the vandals. The share of government shelling became a subject of controversy to determine responsibilities for the destruction of Spain's artistic heritage—of which the English are self-appointed spiritual guardians.

Members of the Leftist parties, slowly emerging from the hiding places into which they were forced by the clerical-fascist terror, rallied their disrupted forces to investigate the inhuman acts which had accompanied the government's repression. Long petitions of protest replete with meticulous and detailed testimony were drawn up, and though these documents could not break through the press censorship they were secretly printed and distributed by the thousands. Public opinion of the Radical Center which had condemned the uprising dared not condone the horrors of the Asturian reconquest. No Spaniard but the most embittered reactionary could feel easy when confronted with descriptions of the Moors pillaging Spanish towns and raping Spanish women. Even though conservatives might refuse to credit the facts about the ingenious cruelties which were practiced on proletarian prisoners, a feeling of shame and disgust crept over them.

Politica Decadente

For the nonce the Radical Center, baptized in blood, and the reactionary C.E.D.A. were cooperating in office to establish the government on a firm foundation while it recuperated from the shock of the October uprising. On November 11, 1934, Gil Robles, now minister of war, made a speech about the necessity for a thorough extirpation of latent revolutionary forces. While the soldiers under his command were wielding the temporal sword, the Catholic demagogue licked the fresh wounds. "The working class should be protected. Wealth must be more evenly distributed. Labor must learn to rely on effective social justice." Early the next year, through the ministrations of the C.E.D.A., relations of intimacy between the Holy See and the Spanish government were re-knotted. Six new bishops were appointed for the salvation of Spanish heretics, and plans for a revision of the constitution were being suited to ecclesiastic taste. The official world was repeatedly told that the Vatican did not in any way mean to interfere in the internal affairs of the Spanish people. Gil Robles' *Acción Popular*, as its name alone proved, was in no wise a Catholic party. The church merely wanted its rights and liberties preserved—"liberties" naturally being used in the traditional medieval sense, meaning franchises and privileges. Only Marxists would point out that the "liberties" under Lerroux-Gil Robles had come to cover all aspects of human existence, from control of the moneybags to the protective domination of the educational system.

In the first weeks of 1935, after the Leftists had apparently been effaced, the struggle for power and the spoils of office within the Right-Center coalition came into the open. All the false crises of the traditional *politica decadente* were re-enacted. Individuals fought over booty amid the unburied corpses of the workers. During interludes of cabinet reorganization the political life of the country was paralyzed for weeks. Prominent Radicals, who represented worldly bourgeois industrialists and had come to appreciate the services of a priest for extreme unction, and chieftains of the C.E.D.A. would meet in secret. Here they manipulated for positions, intrigued over personalities, shaped and reshaped their cliques into novel patterns, and finally emitted the same set of ministers with minor alterations.

In periods of respite from political juggling, constitutional reform was discussed. President Alcalá Zamora wrote long-winded reports in which, after ample investigation, the articles limiting the power of the church, those granting autonomy to the provinces, and those hampering the executive were systematically undermined. The creation of a conservative senate to replace the Tribunal of Constitutional Guarantees was to make Spain safe for herself. Soon, however, the coalition suffered another relapse. Published reports of the Asturian uprising made it difficult for the Radical ministers to sanction the death sentences which had been handed down by the courts-martial. When reprieves were granted to some twenty revolutionaries, the C.E.D.A. and the Agrarians, who felt that only blood could purge this misguided people of sin, dissented and withdrew from the cabinet. Zamora was back at his favorite pastime, consulting party captains. He persistently refused to summon Gil Robles, and Lerroux pulled another *gabinete puente* (bridge cabinet) out of his bag in time for a morbid celebration of the fourth anniversary of the Republic.

Except for the opening of schools with inadequate facilities and the settlement of a number of peasants on parcels of land too limited in area for subsistence, the regime could present no concrete accomplishments. Of the 125 articles of the constitution some had been suspended, others were ignored, and the rest were about to be revised. Leaders of the early years of the Republic were in the Model Prison in Madrid. Official and well-pared statistics of the casualties in the October insurrection had become available. Dead: civilians, 1,051; Civil Guard, 100; other police, 86; army, 98; total, 1,335. Wounded: civilians, 2,051; army and police, 900; total, 2,951. The government bulletins had recorded 30,000 political prisoners, the proceedings of whose trials had become a steady undertone of the regime. While the wives and children of these wretched workers were starving, the most enterprising leaders of the repression were allotted rewards totaling 16,000,000 pesetas. Gil Robles was attending to the rebirth of the church in all its decorative glory. Holy Week in Seville was a revival of an old spectacle with sacred images carried in the public procession, with flowers, candles, and penitent *señoritas.* To complete the medievalism, the government published a special scale of fines in which drunkenness, curses, and songs with political allusions were carefully weighted.

The "state of alarm" was continued through the fall. As soon as moderate Republican deputies were allowed to return to the Chamber scenes of wild disorder regularly disrupted the sessions. Lerroux, in his dotage, indifferent to such demonstrations, seemed destined to die in office, revered by his former enemies. From September 8 to 10 he was in Barcelona receiving homage from Cambó and the *Lliga Catalana.* He had served them well and had been worth his hire. In expansive mood at one banquet Lerroux promised that after the necessary period of suppression had passed he would bestow upon Spain years of peace and felicity. Deafened to other sounds by the applause of the Barcelona industrialists he was installing himself for an extended period.

Corruption

But within a few days after these Catalan feasts, bedlam broke loose. Revelations of corruption in which Spanish cabinet members of the Radical Party were involved, crackled through the country, one stench bomb after another in a pest-ridden political theater. A certain Strauss, in a communication to the president of the Republic, described and documented the relations of high government officials with illegitimate enterprises. He spiced his stories with the ludicrous fact that a "scientific roulette machine" had for six days been set up in the Ministry of the Interior, where it was played in the presence of the Minister, Salazar Alonso, and his departmental chiefs. On October 22 the Cortes, by now a veritable madhouse, discussed the sundry peculations advertised by the informer and attempted to sit in judgment.

After the exchange of lusty and unquotable epithets, men were freed or declared guilty in accordance with some caprice or chance arrangement. The dirty linen of ten Lerroux cabinets was exhibited in the Chamber. On November 28, 1935, the air had not yet cleared when Antonio Nombelo, an ex-inspector of the colonies, in search of vengeance because of his dismissal, reported another financial scandal in which Moreno Calvo, an undersecretary of Lerroux's, played the major role. Documents proved that there had been a conspiracy to defraud the state by the payment of 3,500,000 pesetas to a Barcelona shipowner, Taya. Though the proposed award had never been granted, the fact that Taya was an old friend and protector of Lerroux renewed the agitation of the Strauss affair. During the recounting of these immoralities cabinets toppled and were reset with such frequency that their recording would be meaningless.

The fascist leader, José Primo de Rivera, reveled in the discomfiture of the Radicals. Monarchists achieved new vigor in denouncing the corrupt Republicans. Gil Robles alternated between saving the face of his old ally Lerroux and preparing for a seizure of power on the eve of the Radicals' debacle. President Zamora, in a quandary, summoned one Portela Valladares, the most colorless person he could lay hold of, to assemble a cabinet, and when numerous line-ups collapsed in the process of formation, he granted the new premier a decree of dissolution. Another election, he hoped, would once more vindicate a Center Party in spite of the aspersions cast upon it. The fascist symbols used by the young members of Gil Robles' *Jap* (*Juventud Acción Popular*) troubled him. "Did you see," he exclaimed to his friends, "these boys unfurling their banners and saluting like fascists? That—no . . . neither clenched fists, nor extended palms, nor militias, nor any of that. A Republic of the Center, well in the center (*bien centrada*), with its forces organized in the discipline of the parties which defend it, gracious to the church and supported by the classes of order and a strong army."[11]

Mindful of the constitutional article granting a president only two dissolutions per term, Zamora explicitly referred to his act as the dissolution of the first ordinary Cortes of the Republic. When the president seemed determined to use governmental influence in returning candidates who would serve the fast disintegrating Center, he was bombarded by denunciations on the Right and on the Left. If the elections did not turn in his favor, he was most certain to suffer reprisals, whether the victor were Gil Robles or Azaña. Yet the results of the balloting scheduled for February 16, 1936, were unpredictable, because a host of novel political factors had come into being.

The Origins of the People's Front

The triumph of Hitler, followed by a fascist attempt in France, the massacre of the Austrian workers, and the liquidation of the October uprising in Spain gave the political leaders of the international proletariat pause. Fascism was no purely Roman phenomenon concocted by Mussolini for domestic consumption. Neither was it the inevitable last stand of capitalism, as some German communist writers tended to emphasize, a stage which one even welcomed because it would clarify the air infested with social-democratic deception. Here was a powerful international movement of reaction which called for a counterattack whose lines were not clearly laid down in the classics. The French Communist Party, probably before others, matured to the realization that a broad antifascist front including the middle classes would alone be able to rescue the working-class movement and preserve even that modicum of liberty which the bourgeois democratic state had granted. Naturally, the task of creating amicable relations among Leftist parties which had for years showered each other with the vilest invective could not be accomplished within a few weeks. Propaganda for a United Front, an alliance between the Socialists and the Communists, had been bruited about for many years, usually drowned out by the hymns of hate which these two organizations intoned at each other. Now the United Front was even to be broadened to include bourgeois elements as long as these subscribed to a minimum program of working-class support and pledged themselves to combat fascism. The creation of a People's Front for the defense of democracy became the official policy of the Communist International at its Seventh Congress in the summer of 1935.

In Spain the Left Republicans, the Socialists, and the Communists have vied with each other for the honor of having initiated the new policy. As early as March 13, 1935, Marcelino Domingo, speaking in Catalonia, had called upon Leftist parties to forget their differences and to make common cause. Azaña followed suit. On October 20, 1935, in the Campo de Comillas outside of Madrid he appealed to an audience numbered at 400,000, turning the meeting into a grand demonstration of the growing sentiment of unity on the Left. The Communists—a relatively small party which by February, 1936, had no more than 20,000 members—were more influential in furthering the new People's Front than their numbers would indicate. They first had to crush the spirit of sectarianism which had for long years been fostered in their own ranks; when a purge accomplished this end, they were able to emerge as a powerful and well-knit group. The secretary of the Communist Party, José Diaz, Seville worker, and Dolores Ibarruri, a miner's wife known as La Pasionaria, a moving mass orator, were new figures on the Spanish political scene. Their comparative freedom from murky political alignments gave them unusual popular appeal.

Multiplicity of political attitudes within the Socialist Party made this the largest and least unified group on the Left. Professor Julián Besteiro, an outpost on the party's extreme right, had violently opposed the October insurrection and was not a favorite among the workers. Professor Fernando de los Ríos, though also no partisan of armed rebellion, had nevertheless on April 1, 1935, come to the defense of his party comrades with a lawyer's argument: "The Socialist masses did not rebel against the law. On the contrary, they sacrificed themselves for the law, which the people, under the limited democracy of a bourgeois regime, had given themselves." Such leaders, including Indalecio Prieto, could be lodged within the ideology of the People's Front. Largo Caballero and his followers were less prone to adopt the new attitude. Thirteen months in prison coupled with his recent reading of Marx and Lenin orientated him ever more in the direction of revolutionary purism. When on December 20, 1935, a coalition with the Left Republicans was sanctioned he resigned from the Executive Committee of the Socialist Party. His ideal became a proletarian front, collaboration with the Communists and the Anarchists. Even after January 15, 1936, the day the People's Front pact was finally agreed upon and a common slate of candidates drawn up, Largo Caballero and his left-wing followers kept their eyes turned toward the proletarian masses, away from the middle-class Left Republicans.

The Anarcho-Syndicalists presented an even more thorny problem to the People's Front. Azaña courted them with special appeals, begging them to end the feud and to vote against the fascist candidates. Except for a heterodox syndicalist like Ángel Pestaña, who did venture to accept a place on the common ballot, the majority of the Anarcho-Syndicalist "guides" were cold to the entreaties of the Socialists, Communists, and Left Republicans. On election day, however, these overtures sometimes bore fruit. People's Front candidates were saved by late afternoon orders from Anarcho-Syndicalist union halls, which granted their adherents temporary absolution from party principles and allowed them to go to the polls. In Cadiz, for example, their participation was decisive.

The February Elections, 1936

The Rightist parties now suffered the same internal disruption which had undermined the Left in November, 1933. Gil Robles' *Acción Popular*, Calvo Sotelo's monarchists, and Primo de Rivera's fascists, the Spanish Phalanx, were finding fault with each other for the manner in which they had allowed political power to slip through their fingers. They united only in vilifying Zamora's government candidates and the monsters on the Left. Dead-line alliances patched together between the Rightists and a few Centrists were usually unsuccessful. Toward the end of the campaign leaders of the Right, though they continued to broadcast their faith in an overwhelming victory, were well aware of an impending disaster. In desperation Ángel Herrera, the *éminence grise* of *Acción Popular*, made the rounds of the English, American, and German embassies, confiding to the foreigners his fears of a Marxist triumph. He hoped that after his communication the ambassadors would intercede with Alcalá Zamora so that governmental influence might bear in the right direction.

The election campaign itself was the most hectic Spain had ever experienced. Candidates tried to cover the most remote towns. Radios rasped forth political speeches over the sleepiest of village squares. The walls of ancient churches and municipal buildings afforded ideal expanses for posters in which the Spanish genius excelled. *U.H.P.* and the red hammer and sickle were painted on conspicuous parts of holy statues. "Asturias and Amnesty!" was the battle cry of the Left. Drawings of haggard women and children extending plaintive arms to men behind prison bars; graphic depiction of the fascist whips lashing the backs of chained workers; and caricatures of the pear-shaped head of Gil Robles were outstanding features of the Leftist gallery. The Right retorted with: "Against the revolution and its accomplices!" In its posters the map of Spain was gripped by the hairy hand of Marxism. In the provinces the reactionaries could rely upon their old stand-bys, the village priests and the *caciques*, who warned that the People's Front meant communism, sacrilege, church burning, and the nationalization of women. The homeliest of slogans were the most efficacious. One village wall bore the memorable device: "Death to Azaña! Long live God!"

As the election returns were being recorded on February **17**, the government radio station, as if it could mystically alter the decision, kept broadcasting its own Right-Center victory. Catalonia, where the *Esquerra* (Left) won with a crushing majority, brought the first news of the real tendency of the ballot. In Madrid, Azaña routed Gil Robles; chieftains of the Right and Center, Lerroux, Cambó, Martínez de Velasco, were not returned. Faced with a People's Front landslide civil governors and local authorities abandoned their offices without waiting for a regular transfer of power. The lords of the reaction trembled. What would the masses do now that their hour of triumph had arrived? What bloody vengeance were they preparing? But instead of terror, a holiday spirit of restrained joy prevailed in the cities and towns of the land. At the behest of their leaders the people of Madrid who had filled the Puerto del Sol in a spontaneous mass demonstration retired in peace to resume their normal work.

On February 19, Portela Valladares handed in his resignation and Azaña was called to the presidential palace. On several occasions since 1933, whenever Zamora had called Azaña for consultation, the Republican leader had scorned the summons. When he came to that palace again, Don Manuel had vowed, he would enter "breaking down the doors."

NOTES

1. Adolphe de Falgairolle, *L'Espagne en République*, pp. 135, 139, Paris, 1933.
2. Quoted from P. McBride, "Gil Robles and Spanish Politics," *The Irish Monthly*, vol. 42, p. 203, 1934. See Maurice Lewandowski, "M. Gil Robles," *Revue des Deux Mondes*, vol. 27, 8ᵉ période, pp. 860 ff., 1935.
3. McBride, *loc. cit.*, p. 207.

4. In 1935 Juan Castrillo Santos, a conservative Republican, thus summarized Radical tactics: " . . . first, receive the electoral support of the C.E.D.A.; then collaborate with the C.E.D.A. in the government; finally support the C.E.D.A. in parliament in order that it may govern." *Cuatro años de experiencia republicana*, 1931–1935, p. 207, Madrid, 1935.

5. Manuel Grossi, a worker, one of the leaders of the revolt in the Asturias, has emphasized the importance of the German example in his graphic diary, *La insurrección de Asturias*, pp. 17–18, Barcelona, 1935: "The Ceda, no! The participation of the Ceda in the government would be the first official victory of fascism. To accept this without resistance, without a struggle, . . . it would be complicity. . . . The bitter experience of the German workers was present in everyone's mind. This experience the Spanish workers would not repeat."

6. Antonio Ramos Oliveira, *La Revolución española de octubre*, Madrid, 1935, quotes on the flyleaf Gil Robles' speech of December 15, 1934: "I was certain that our reaching power would unleash a revolutionary movement."

7. Luis Araquistáin, "The October Revolution in Spain," *Foreign Affairs*, vol. 13, p. 258, 1935.

8. A communist leaflet issued after the defeat outlined causes for the failure and drew lessons for future action. "Because . . . the political and organizational preparations were insufficient, because its program was not made known to the whole of the working masses. . . . The fact was ignored that revolution is not made but organized." *International Press Correspondence*, November 3, 1934, vol. 14, p. 1485.

9. See the analysis of events in Joaquín Maurín, *Hacia la segunda revolución*, Madrid, 1935.

10. For the conclusions of an Englishwoman's investigation see Leah Manning, *What I Saw in Spain*, London, 1935.

11. Quoted from *Energías, Síntesis de las actividades nacionales*, p. 110, Madrid, 1936.

Chapter VIII

THE WAY OF THE PEOPLE'S FRONT

The February election conducted under the aegis of a government frankly hostile to socialist reforms had given the People's Front proper more than 4 million votes, about one half of the total number of ballots cast.[1] In addition, hundreds of thousands of nonvoting anarcho-syndicalists, whose bizarre philosophy made them the sphinx-like element of Spanish politics, could be counted on the Left. It is true the People's Front did not prove itself an expression of the unanimous will of all Spain, harassed as that will was by mystic images from the past, freshly dressed in the uniforms of modern fascism. But the People's Front might have *become* the ideal of so vast a body of workers, peasants, intellectuals, and sons of the lower middle class that no exponent of the old regime would have dared to defy the Republic.

The People's Front came in like a lion; it soon found itself confined in a political cage whose bars, though rusty, still condemned it to pace up and down in impotent bewilderment. Throughout May and June there was a feeling of utter helplessness in governmental circles. Superficially, life in cities and towns appeared normal—theaters, restaurants, bullfights; yet one's ears did not have to be pricked high to hear the clanking of fascist arms. From the very day of the February election up to the fateful eighteenth of July, a military rebellion was common table talk.

On February 16 the undismayed faces of Spanish reactionaries peered from behind the gigantic windows of their clubhouses in the Calle de Alcalá; they were still there on the eve of July 18. On the outskirts of cities like Córdoba rose villages populated by wretched agricultural laborers who lived in hovels constructed of tin and cardboard boxes. They were still there on the eve of July 18. "What has the Republic given you to eat?" was the ominous question in 1933. "What has the People's Front given

151

you to eat?" was the telling blow in 1936.   Had the Republican
leaders forgotten their first harrowing experience in 1931–1933?
Had they learned nothing?   The scale of emotions from pretentious optimism to dank disillusion had before required more
than two years to traverse; now they could flutter over the same
scale in a few months, for they seemed to know the way.

Could the leaders of the People's Front forge the Spanish
nation into a willful community, or were they inevitably destined
to lose themselves in that labyrinth of economic and social
problems which time, the Republic's adversaries, and its friends
had laid out?   Doctrines were abundant, brevets to prosperity
and happiness.   Millions of workers and peasants were formless
matter, malleable.   The church was fast losing its hold, and these
millions vaguely desired the Revolution.   But the Revolution,
mild and temperate, or the Revolution, violent and tempestuous,
would have to reveal itself in deeds.   The peasants had forsaken
one credo; they were not eager to embrace the weak vessel which
contained another.

"If on the morrow of the elections we had taken Gil Robles
and Lerroux and a few of the generals who led the army in the
Asturias and lined them up against the wall, that would have
meant something," was the unguarded reflection of one Spanish
Leftist.   In so doing the People's Front would have immediately
sacrificed the good will of international democratic opinion
and would have tossed off the laurel of legality.   Yet perhaps
it would have been prudent to forfeit, and value at naught, that
good will ere it lived to reappear at a European council table
in the guise of a nonintervention committee.

The Impeachment of Alcalá Zamora

The initial pact of the People's Front parties had stipulated
that in the event of an electoral victory only Left Republicans
would sit in the cabinet.   While the common program of reform
was being executed the Socialists and the Communists agreed
to support their allies in the Cortes.   On the People's Front
lists of candidates the Left Republicans had been allotted more
places than their due in order to give the movement a moderate
tenor.   Hence one anomaly stared the country in the face as
soon as Azaña published the names of his ministers: the masses
were Socialist, Communist, and Anarchist, while their apparent

representatives in the cabinet were bourgeois Left Republicans with no popular party behind them. Except for Azaña himself and the Minister of Public Works, Quiroga, there were no outstanding personalities.

On February 20 Azaña addressed himself to the people, recommending "patience" as he had a few years previously. For the benefit of the defeated parties he added that no one would be persecuted who maintained himself within the pale of the law. A few decrees, approved by the Permanent Representative Committee of the Cortes, were immediately promulgated. Thousands of prisoners of the October insurrection were amnestied, a formal sanction in many instances of the freedom which the people had already granted the prisoners on the day after the election by opening the jails. Her autonomous rights were restored to Catalonia. Workers who had been dismissed during political strikes declared after January 1, 1934, were to be rehired by their employers. Dispossessed tenants (*yunteros*) were to be returned to their land.

From the opening session of March 15 to April 2 the Cortes debated the legality of various elections, refusing to seat the Rightist candidates of Granada and Cuenca, though passing over the dark practices which surrounded the choice of the Monarchist Calvo Sotelo in his little fief of Orense. The Cortes acted with comparative haste because a major operation, the impeachment of Alcalá Zamora, was to be its first task. The People's Front had decided that it could not breathe freely while a tacit collaborator of the repression in the Asturias sat in the presidential palace. Zamora refused to resign. Thereupon the parties of the People's Front drew forth articles 81 and 82 of the Spanish constitution, which elaborated the impeachment procedure. Indalecio Prieto became the people's advocate, and with fine logic proved that the president, in dissolving the last Cortes, had intended to constitute himself the sole arbiter of the nation's destiny. The third Cortes of a presidential term had the constitutional right to examine the conditions under which the second had been dissolved, and when an absolute majority of the deputies declared that the president had used his prerogatives unnecessarily, the head of the state was impeached.

Sardonic humor marked a procedure which doomed a president for having made possible the victory of the People's Front; but the

formal weapon was unimportant.   "If the majority were egoist,"
said Prieto, "it would maintain S. Alcalá Zamora in his position,
because that would in itself insure the indissolubility of Parliament until the expiration of its mandate.   But that would indicate a lack of political perspicacity."   The Right was not
overzealous in defense of a president who had lost them their
majority.   The Center could only whine: "A lie, a lie," in the
accepted Spanish manner.   According to the constitution the
new Speaker of the Cortes, Martínez Barrio, was automatically
raised to the provisional presidency, and Zamora was invited to
vacate his palace.   In the streets of the capital this incident,
which would have aroused fervent public interest in another
democracy, passed unnoticed.   It was an obvious act of house
cleaning.

Azaña's Presidential Regime

Late in April, Spain, the Right abstaining, voted for presidential electors, who meeting together with the Cortes were to
choose a new president.   On May 10 Azaña, to the astonishment
of many of his friends, bade farewell to the political arena and
accepted the presidency bestowed upon him by an overwhelming
majority.   During the inauguration the pompous ceremonies
which had marked Zamora's entrance into the presidential palace
were repeated for the candidate of the People's Front.

The peregrinations of government officials could not be of more
than passing interest to the Spanish masses.   They were not
invited to the grand banquets in the presidential palace, where
feasts were illuminated by candelabra, and braided flunkeys
moved to and fro among flapping coattails.   For them there was
work to be done.   Throughout the land the fascists were beginning to snipe at Republicans, and workers in protest were declar-
ing general strikes.   When the relations between a monastery
and a fascist band came to light, the vengeance of the people
spared neither the structure nor the ancient manuscripts which
it housed.   Azaña, while still prime minister, officially dissolved
the fascist leagues and withdrew pensions, as he had once
threatened, from those retired army officers who had since
dabbled in politics.   But such preventive measures, often
inadequately executed because enemies of the people lurked in

every department of the civil administration and military establishment, failed to thwart the cunning of the assassin's arm.

The new premier, Casares Quiroga, though known for his energy and administrative ability, seemed to be reliving those wild months when, as Minister of the Interior, he sat in Azaña's first Republican cabinet. In his opening speech before the Cortes he defied the fascists, threatened them in unguarded language, and announced rather cryptically that he was not opposed to social revolution. In private conversations he intimated that profound changes were inevitable. But in the streets it was said that he was a consumptive devouring himself in an impossible undertaking, for the rest of his cabinet were of dubious vintage. Barcia, the minister of foreign affairs, was suspect because of the relations which he maintained with the *cacique* of his province in Almería. Bernardo Giner de los Ríos, minister of communications, and Barnés, minister of public instruction, were both scions of those spiritual fathers of the Spanish Republic who had organized the Free Institute of Education. They retained the intellectual outlook of Spanish anticlericals of the nineties and were aliens among the modern proletariat. At moments they regretted their revolutionary temerity. Lluhí, the Catalan, who occupied the Ministry of Labor, enjoyed the sympathy of some Socialists, though he was impotent in the midst of strikes which broke upon each other like waves dashing against a rocky shore. Reactionaries in the lower ranks of his own bureaucracy were not to be trusted; in many quarters they were blamed for the prolongation throughout the spring of a strike of elevator men and janitors harassing middle-class Madrid.

Spain's troubled finances were in the hands of Ramos, who, it was rumored, relied upon the advice of Viñuales, an aged professor of economics connected with the Banco Urquijo. Perhaps the most important figure in the financial structure of the government, however, was Flores de Lemus, a director of one of the ministerial bureaus, who since the early twenties had framed most of the economic measures of the various cabinets. A conservative educated at German universities, with a cynical contempt for politics, he elected to act as a factotum for ministers of finance who knew nothing about their office. He struggled with the Stabilizing Fund for the People's Front as he had for Lerroux; he tried to bolster a falling peseta in 1936 as he had for Primo de

Rivera and Berenguer in 1929–1931. A few days before the fascist rebellion, in the red plush anteroom of his office and in the midst of an intricate account of his heroic combat with international financiers, Flores de Lemus referred nonchalantly to the possibility of a military uprising. Undersecretaries in other offices were of the same caliber.

The Left Republican ministers were obviously not the dominant figures of the People's Front. The living issues of the Republic were not solved in their administrative chambers nor were they expounded from the blue bench of the Cortes. The political drama of the People's Front was enacted in the meeting halls of the workers' parties, the Socialists, the Anarchists, and the Communists. The formal program of the People's Front, which for the purpose of including certain republican bourgeois elements had carefully sidetracked a specific labor platform, could never nourish a vigorous mass movement. Azaña, the president, who fancied himself the secret mediator of the internal disputes of a Leftist Republic, and the lesser lights in the ministries did not inspire blind confidence on the part of the people. Hence at the outset the bourgeois Left Republicans sought the collaboration of the Socialist Party, that good old band of reformers who had once agreed to build a new Spain for the economic benefit of the greatest number without ramming through too many ancient edifices. In shouldering the responsibilities of office along with the Left Republicans the Socialist leaders, and perhaps the masses over whom they had influence, would realize the hardships of the task before them and would be more lenient in their criticisms. The October uprising of 1934 had left its impress upon many Left Republicans; they had learned the mannerisms of militant speech. But they were soon appalled by the undercurrents in the Socialist Party. They trembled at the sight of a two-headed Cerberus into which it had been metamorphosed.

The months before the rebellion of July 18, 1936, were spent by the Socialist Party in airing a violent internecine quarrel which shook the country, as all other political factions on the Left stood by awaiting the outcome before they could define their own positions. Should the Socialist Party accept a cabinet position as it had in 1931 or should it not? This became the immediate bone of contention between two factions, and soon revealed deep divergences in social theory and practice which seemed to be leading

inevitably to party schism. Whether or not to collaborate with
the bourgeois Left—the standard dilemma of socialist parties
ever since it was posed in France by Millerand in the late nineteenth century—was being debated once again, with an array of
arguments which had become hackneyed in England, Germany,
Belgium, and the Scandinavian countries. Though the existence
of the People's Front introduced a number of novel elements in
the Spanish compound, most of the speeches delivered during
the quarrel and most of the editorials written with grand flourishes read like translations.

The Prietists

Indalecio Prieto, once known as a Centrist Socialist, led in the
advocacy of the moderate line which involved participation in
the Left Republican cabinet. Professors like Fernando de los
Ríos and the bureaucracy of the party aligned themselves with
him. The left wing, under Largo Caballero, derived its support
from the *U.G.T.*, the socialist trade-union federation. It violently
denounced the proposed entrance of the party leaders into another
coalition cabinet. The organs of the two rivals, *El Socialista*,
the official party newspaper siding with Prieto, and *Claridad*, the
new daily founded by Caballero's friends, covered each other with
opprobrium. When the followers of the two camps cast doubts
on each other's personal integrity they drew shouts of joy from
the monarchist *A.B.C.*, which playfully agreed with the accusations of both factions.

The abstract arguments with which Prieto and Fernando de los
Ríos garnished their policy soon became far less important than
the interpretations of their actions by the bourgeoisie on the one
side and the proletariat on the other. Prieto personally remained
a rather sentimental self-made man, who loved his people and
his land; he was still a Socialist without benefit of Marxism.
He impressed observers with the tremendous vitality which
shook his corpulent body—a possible strong man for Spain.
His attitude on the eve of the Franco rebellion and the energy
with which he has since served the Loyalist cause in organizing
the defense have dispelled accusations once leveled against him.
Nevertheless, in May and June, talk of a republican dictatorship
under Prieto was rampant, and the rumors robbed him of popular
support. Spain's industrialists were looking about for a Thiers,

some ex-Radical or preferably some ex-Socialist leader who would stem the tide of revolution through his influence on the lower strata of society. First Lerroux had been their man; for a while, with little discernment, they had turned towards Azaña; now that Prieto was in favor of collaborating with the bourgeois republican regime they were considering him for the post. Industrialists invited Don Indalecio to address their assemblies, and the bourgeois newspaper *El Sol* almost killed him with flattery when it praised his Bilbao speech as the pronouncement of a true patriot.

To the Spanish worker who was for the first time listening to the call of revolutionary socialism, the frank opening sentence of Prieto's May First speech in Cuenca must have sounded peculiar: "As I get on in years, I, once an internationalist, feel myself more and more profoundly Spanish." Time and again Prieto emphasized the country's economic problems; first he would raise Spanish economy from its present low station, and then the social revolution would come of itself. In order that the vast plans of economic development and the great systems of water power which he projected might be realized, the working-class parties of the Left would have to join hands with the bourgeois Republicans. A violent revolution which might destroy democracy would in Spain's impoverished state, he warned, bring neither socialism nor communism. Anarchy would result, a haphazard disintegration of forces which would belie the libertarian's ideal. The workers would be the first to suffer. Spasmodic uprisings and intermittent strikes were creating an atmosphere of uneasiness. In such an environment was fascism bred. The People's Front in power should proceed with measures of reform. . . . Thus Prieto appeared as the leader of a bourgeois revolution, a radical liberal whose radicalism consisted in his desire to hasten the tempo of economic transformation.

The Followers of Largo Caballero

Caballero and his friends, despairing of any effective social change in collaboration with a cabinet of Left Republicans, became the heralds of a proletarian revolution. They articulated the desire of the millions who belonged to the General Union of Workers (*U.G.T.*). Many of its Socialist and Communist members had been killed during the October insurrection; thousands of the most active trade-unionists had been herded into jails where they were subjected to inquisitorial persecutions. Their homes had been ransacked, their papers destroyed. When the amnesty restored the victims to the light of day and returned them to their former employment, the benevolent decree did not wipe away the memory of their sufferings. At the sight of employers who had often been instrumental in effecting their arrest their hatred was constantly rekindled. The People's Front was victorious; but they still earned starvation wages so that their "bosses might ride about in automobiles and drink their *apéritifs*."

By Largo Caballero's side were two brilliant journalists, Luis Araquistáin and Álvarez del Vayo, foreign correspondents who had been stationed in many European countries and who were endowed with sophisticated political sensibilities. Araquistáin, it should be remembered, had been the Spanish ambassador to Germany in 1933, and he had stored up a wealth of experience. Álvarez del Vayo was a devoted admirer of Soviet Russia. These two men were fast becoming the official theoreticians for the revolutionary Left Socialists. Their newspaper *Claridad* and their monthly *Leviatán* disseminated the phraseology of revolutionary Marxism. Many Spaniards for the first time were reading actual excerpts from Karl Marx on the class war, passages which expressed with force and conciseness what they had been feeling. Araquistáin was the man of letters, no mass leader. Caballero was the popular figure, apotheosized as the Spanish Lenin.

The intellectuals among the Left Socialists could not help feeding upon the historical analogies of the Russian Revolution, sometimes biting off larger morsels than they could digest. Superficial similarities were striking: a backward country, an ignorant peasantry, a class-conscious city proletariat which, though small in number, was as militant in action as the industrial workers of Petrograd. The uprising of 1934 in the Asturias was the dress rehearsal, equivalent to the Russian Revolution of 1905. The Left Republicans were Kerenskys of a sort, who had to be supported temporarily, as a "rope supports one who is hanged." The Spanish Revolution was destined to follow—a parallel for the October Revolution of 1917. Such literary images fired imagination. Spain had no war crisis, hence the cumulative effect of strikes would have to serve the purpose in creating a prerevolutionary temper and in revealing the extent to which the administrative organs of government had broken down.

Though Caballero was not always in agreement with the plans of the revolutionary *littérateurs*, he was slowly being forced into a similar position by the struggle within the Socialist Party. Collaboration with the government meant to him a repetition of the 1931–1933 experience. It would necessarily extinguish the revolutionary fire of the masses, as identical socialist tactics in other countries attested with a mountain of evidence. The Socialists must remain pure; when they seized power it would not be with bourgeois bells dangling at their skirts. They could not disillusion the masses once again by promising them social ameliorations which were not in their power to effect under a bourgeois economy. Throughout May and June Caballero orated almost every Sunday in the great bullrings of Spanish provincial capitals, arousing a frenzy of enthusiasm as he expounded, in what seemed to be verbatim quotations from Marx, that the bourgeois system must collapse and that class war was inevitable. He pointed out that the particular form of bourgeois government, conservative or People's Front, was of little import so far as the living standard of the worker was concerned, because the bourgeois economy was based on deadly competition. Only the working class, when vested with the fullness of state power, would be able to eradicate the evils from which it was suffering.

But what of the People's Front and the fascist menace? To this Caballero replied that the government need have no fears. Constructive measures of the People's Front would be supported in the Cortes by the Left Socialists; in the streets, should fascism dare show its hideous face, the Spanish proletariat would arise to batter it. The masses were still the government's most faithful protectors. *Claridad* provided a formula for Caballero's policy: "Diversity in Unity." The Left Socialists were part of the People's Front as far as its limited program was concerned; for the rest, they were an independent group with liberty of action and freedom of criticism.

Thus Caballero inveighed against the government's criminal negligence in retaining fascists in the bureaucracy and against the remnants of the old regime which cluttered administrative machinery and hindered the enforcement of those reforms which had already been passed. In its polemics *Claridad* knew no meas-

ure. It bandied about the word "fascist" with the same reck-
lessness as had the Communists prior to 1935, and men who had
sacrificed their lives in the Asturias uprising were confounded
with Lerroux and Gil Robles. Specific incidents added physical
violence to the ideological disputes. During the meeting of the
electoral college which made Azaña president of the Republic,
Araquistáin, editor of *Claridad*, gave Zugazagoitia, editor of
El Socialista, a resounding slap. Sympathetic observers questioned whether a group which heaped such contumely upon its
allies could at a given signal fall into an embrace.

An analysis of the function of Caballero's agitation must take
cognizance of the impending fascist conflict. Evaluated in
retrospect, these fiery demonstrations seem to have fulfilled a
purpose of great import. If the proletarian masses of Spain had
not been stirred to a pitch of revolutionary ardor they might
not have responded so heroically as they did to the challenge of
armed troops. After all, the millions of solid and orderly
German Socialists and Communists had accepted Hitler with
many a whimper, but without a struggle. Would a well-
disciplined People's Front, perhaps *à la française*, have been
able to rouse the unarmed masses to storm fortified barracks?
Did not the revolutionary image evoked by Caballero inspire
that self-sacrifice which destroyed the fascist dream of a two
weeks' parade through Spain?

The Socialist Executive Committee, under Prieto's influence,
succeeded in postponing the party congress until October, 1936,
despite the accusations of the Caballero group, pressing for an
immediate anticollaborationist decision from the membership,
that this was a Centrist coup. Prieto intended to use the
interval to address vast bullring meetings throughout Spain—
to rally the masses to his own standard before they were irre-
vocably lost to Caballero. But Prieto was forced to abandon
his speech-making after a pathetic appearance at Ecija on May
31. At the very entrance to the meeting he and his lieutenants,
Belarmino Tomás and González Peña, were greeted with banners
in praise of Caballero and his organ *Claridad*. No sooner had
Tomás begun to speak than he was interrupted with an incessant
repetition of the revolutionary cry *U.H.P.!* In desperation he
retorted: "True Socialists would not come to a meeting in this
spirit. . . . I risked my life, with a gun in my hand, for fifteen

days in the Asturias." *U.H.P.!* resounded through the arena.
When Peña, Prieto, and Tomás had been in the Asturias these
three letters had been whispered in secret hide-outs as the pass-
word of the revolutionaries.   Now the election cry of the Left,
it was hurled in the faces of the same leaders who had once pronounced it at the peril of their lives.   "You have no right to
that cry," Tomás exclaimed.   "It is ours.   It is ours!"   Frantic,
he tried to continue, but in vain; some one had cut the wires of
the loud-speaker.   Prieto intervened and the meeting was disrupted.   Six policemen were hurt protecting the former heroes
of the Asturias as they fled the bullring.   Thereafter Prieto
made no more public speeches and restrained his natural volu-
bility even before newspapermen.   Like a Socialist Achilles, he
sulked in his summer home in Alicante.   It was said that he was
biding his time, allowing Caballero's movement to spend its
force.   Every few weeks *El Liberal*, Prieto's Bilbao newspaper,
issued a sibylline warning about the fascist enemy.

The Advance of the Communist Party

Caballero's alternative for collaboration with the bourgeois
Left Republicans was the unification of proletarian parties, the
Socialists, the Communists, and the Anarcho-Syndicalists.   His
relations with the Communists were the most amicable, for the
young Spanish Communist Party was quick to grasp the opportunity of associating itself with the masses who supported
Caballero.   The youth organizations of the Left Socialists and
the Communists merged, and the demonstrations of their
common militia frightened Right Socialists and bourgeois
Republicans.   Yet from the beginning both groups, apparently
identical in their social doctrines, had two divergent outlooks
on the policy to be pursued.   The Communists, with a membership of about 20,000 in February, were slowly expanding to the
150,000 mark reached in July.   Undoubtedly their influence
was far greater than that exerted by their 16 representatives in the
Cortes.   Secretly they were rather lukewarm toward Caballero's
tactics.   But they carefully avoided expressing any overt opinion
about the schism within the Socialist Party, and they guarded
themselves against overworking their revolutionary phraseology.
At the same mass meetings where Caballero would intone
his philosophy of the class war, José Diaz, in the spirit of his

party's interpretation of the People's Front, would call upon the
Left Republicans for greater militancy in their policies of reform
and reconstruction. He demanded the forty-hour week, higher
wages, unemployment compensation, and more efficient enforcement of the agrarian law. He urged specific measures against
the Spanish Phalanx, against reactionary elements among the
Civil Guards, against conspiratorial associations of employers
who were closing their factories, against brazen industrialists
who ignored the decisions of the *jurados mixtos* (boards of arbitration), against the Jesuits who still held the reins of the educational
system. He favored more free schools, larger allowances for
physical culture, and more extensive public works projects.
The Communist Party organ, *Mundo Obrero*, continually ham-
mered away at the government that the fascist menace had not
vanished, that there were still arsenals of arms in the country,
and that officials were not vigilant enough in checking the export
of pesetas by grandees and monks. The language of Communist newspapers, however, was always discreet in its censure of
the government. This was no period for any abstract expositions
of the "dictatorship of the proletariat," the Communists reasoned, when the country had not yet experienced even the
bourgeois revolution. Only specific measures could definitively
win over the peasantry to the side of the Republic, ending the
vacillation of every new election.

Far from alienating mild Republican sentiment, the Communists tried to establish firm lines of contact between the anti-
fascist writers of France and those of Spain. A steady stream
of French novelists, like André Malraux and Jean-Richard Bloch,
was sent across the Pyrenees to aid in solidifying an anti-
fascist bloc of Spanish intellectuals which would counterbalance
the weight of the reactionary stylists who turned phrases for
A.B.C. and *El Debate*. The poet Rafael Alberti and his wife
María Teresa, two youthful Communists, gathered about them
a circle of intellectuals who strove to break through the somber
cast of Spanish pessimist thought molded by Unamuno and his
generation.

In every sphere the Communists were extending their influence
on behalf of a strong People's Front. Caballero's attitude,
however, presented to them a curious situation. For daily action
they would have preferred a militant united movement to

Caballero's sectarianism and phrasemongering.   In some respects even Prieto's Centrist viewpoint was more in harmony with the new Communist policy than was the revolutionary purism of the Left Socialists.   On the other hand, Prieto had come to represent only a restricted section of the Socialist Party bureaucracy, and the Communists felt it their duty to maintain, above all else, contact with a mass organization.   The public demonstrations of unanimity between Caballero and the Communists thus remained somewhat factitious.   José Diaz, secretary of the Communist Party, during a private discussion of the complex trends within the People's Front early in July, 1936, assented to "infantile leftist" as the proper term for Caballero's tendencies.

Communist propaganda reached the tiniest villages, mere agglomerations of white huts.   Representatives of the party from Madrid were welcomed by the peasant officials of these municipalities with the sign of the clenched fist and the greeting *Salud*.   In defiance of the village priest, meetings of the Communist Party were held in the squares.   María Teresa Alberti's speech at one of the meetings of the townspeople of Cervera del Llana, a village of 1,200 inhabitants in Cuenca, showed the care with which the Communists were slowly breaking down the traditional conservatism of the peasants and were binding them to the city proletariat:

We come to you with cordial greetings from the workers of Madrid. We know that you are subject to the oppression of the *cacique* and of the aristocrat.   Does it have to be so?   I want to tell you how the peasants live in Russia, and we can compare the way they live with the way you are now living.   I know what the bourgeois newspaper writers are telling you.   They say that in Russia there is no family life. They tell you that the peasants have been robbed of their land.   But I come to tell you that all this is a lie which the bourgeois press is spreading in order to keep you in your present state.   They did not destroy the family in Russia when they provided for the health of the children.   The condition of women has been improved, not by lowering them in the eyes of men, but rather by showing an ever greater respect towards them.   The Communist system has provided for schools.   It brings theatres and the cinema and libraries to all the people. It has fought against disease, against typhoid which every year robs you of your children.   It has given the peasants new machines to make their labor easier. . . . This is what communism has done in Russia and this is what it can do for you. . . . When you hear of striking workers, support them, because the workers in the city and the peasants in the country form one unit, one group, one class. . . . Long live the People's Front!

In this manner the Communists hoped to canalize the vague desires for revolution which animated the peasants. Time alone was necessary, time to cover the outlying districts where the *cacique*'s sway had never been challenged, time for the leadership of a new party to assert itself. Every week that the reaction postponed its blow brought new men to swell the ranks of the Communist Party. Left Socialists, Caballero's own followers, disgusted by the strife within their party, bewildered by its formlessness, often chose to ally themselves with the Communists, whose superior discipline could control their revolutionary action. The sons of old anarchists, attracted perhaps by an almost military efficiency, abandoned the libertarian ideology of their fathers to join the young party. Communist prestige grew steadily in the General Union of Workers, and secretly undermined the influence of Caballero in his own fortress.

Ultimately, when months after the rebellion in May, 1937, the Communists deemed it advisable to oust the chieftain because of his inefficiency and arrogance, they could smoothly dispatch their mission without disrupting the People's Front government. As a result of its international connections, the Communist Party was able to draw upon a wealth of revolutionary experience, which made it possible to coordinate the details of a confused political moment. The party thus attained a marked practical superiority over less disciplined and less informed Leftist parties. The way the raw Spanish Communist Party, with the aid of political advisers from the Comintern and with material succor from Soviet Russia, succeeded in winning thousands of adherents in the midst of the struggle against Franco is a tribute to the technical capacities of the national and international leadership of the movement. No Spanish Lenin came to the fore; hence the effectiveness of the rank and file is the more striking.

Anarchist Intransigence

During the weeks before July 18, the Right Socialist intellectuals looked askance at the growing intimacy between Caballero, the Communists, and the Anarchists.   Fernando de los Ríos, in answering a pointed question about the possible relations between the latter groups and the Right Socialists replied with professorial finality: "With the Communists we can go so far. With the Anarchists we cannot go.   They do not recognize the law.   They are outlaws.   A chasm separates socialism from anarchy in its view of history and philosophy."   *El Socialista,* in the tone of a weeping old lady, bewailed the humiliation of Indalecio Prieto at Ecija and summoned the shadow of Pablo Iglesias to deplore with the Socialists the sorry state of their party.   In answer to insults leveled at its leader the Right Socialist organ indulged in malevolent and catty reflections. Where had *Claridad* obtained money to purchase the tremendous printing presses which it was running?   Had a bank controlled by Catholic reactionaries contributed the funds?   Was not one of Caballero's favorites a certain Carlos Baráibar, once a minion of the Jesuits?

   On the relations between the People's Front and the Anarchists the rival factions within the Socialist Party seemed irreconcilable. In his orations Caballero had gone more than halfway in making overtures to the Anarcho-Syndicalists.   On May 24, in a speech at Cadiz, he tried to prove that there was no fundamental doctrinal difference between the militant Socialist of the General Union of Workers and the Anarcho-Syndicalist of the National Federation of Labor.   One of the Syndicalists, Ballester, while speaking on the same platform, had intimated that they diverged on their conception of the state, and while Caballero's answer would not have appeased a political theorist, it drew salvos from his audience.   "We too say that the bourgeois state must disappear because the bourgeois state is nothing more than an organization of oppression against a class, our class.   And when this class triumphs establishing a new regime, and when the regime perfects itself, the state *per se* will disappear.   This is the doctrine of the General Union of Workers."

   Thus Caballero harmonized his newly discovered Marxist-Leninist conception of the withering away of the state with the Syndicalist hatred of all its forms and institutions.   Yet ardently as the Left Socialists and even the Communists courted the Anarcho-Syndicalists through Workers' Alliances and sundry committees the intransigent revolutionaries could not be won over to full cooperation in a Proletarian Front. The activities of the Anarcho-Syndicalists during these months would make even the most sympathetic chronicler despair. The National Confederation of Labor, after the Saragossa Congress of May, 1936, transferred its headquarters from Barcelona to Madrid and under the lenient regime of the People's Front renewed its agitation with vigor in Socialist as well as in Communist strongholds. The strikes of the Syndicalists honeycombed the country. Every industry in its turn was convulsed. When the General Union of Workers participated with members of the Syndicalist Federation on a common strike policy, the more violent body invariably swept the workers along with it and dictated the strategy of class combat. Government officials, Prieto, even Caballero, sent appeals to the country to moderate the strike movement, but the mass of workers were desperate and were prepared to follow the most ardent leaders.

In this maze of economic conflicts it would, however, be unjust to lay the responsibility for all the strikes upon the Syndicalists. Many of the movements reported in the international press as strikes were actually lockouts or the direct result of employers' provocation in pursuit of a course laid out by the fascists. Nevertheless, one should not minimize the ire of the Anarcho-Syndicalists once they realized the weakness of the People's Front. There was every reason to believe that they would continue their "strike gymnastics" until the dawn of the Great Day. The tormenting problem remained: How was the government to react to the unrest if it became violent? How would the Right Socialists, if they joined the cabinet? As long as these were mere strikes, the government could affect a pose of economic neutrality and warn the Civil Guard that they must not attack the people without authorization. When the movement assumed serious political proportions, however, would the elect of the People's Front repress the uprising of the people as had Lerroux?

Caballero's attempt at conciliating the Anarcho-Syndicalists failed, and a tragic clash at Malaga between members of the two labor federations opened an old wound. For a few days, until the Civil Guard reestablished order, there were intermittent assassinations of leaders in both camps. News spread throughout the land; an embittered Communist worker, on reading the headlines, shouted: "They're all fascists! We'll have to kill them first!" Throughout the months of June the Left Socialist group seemed to be pulling in its reins, while the Anarcho-Syndicalist newspaper headlines blasted away. "Hunger cannot wait!" cried *El Sindicalista*. "The Revolution, yea!" was the cover of another sheet.

Government censorship tried to suppress the news of strikes and assassinations because the ministers feared the contagion of violence. Copy for daily newspapers had to be rushed to the official press bureau for examination; the deleted sections appeared as blank space or with broken type. The Paris *Temps*, arriving a few days late in Madrid, was often more informative than the newspapers of the Spanish capital. Only when one gathered a batch of provincial papers and turned to the pages entitled *Social Conflicts* could one fully realize the scope of labor discontent for which there were no official statistics. If the civil governor of a province felt so inclined he closed the Syndicalist *Casa del Pueblo* (House of the People: Trade-union Hall), for the severity of the disciplinary measures against Syndicalist strikers varied with individual officials. The Anarchists were confirmed in their principles. "The people and the government," wrote *Tierra y Libertad* (*Land and Liberty*), "are two irreconcilable entities. We too might like to be deputies and city councillors enjoying all the advantages which these positions may offer. But we affirm again that God and the devil cannot be served at the same time; one cannot be both for the government and for the people."

In the meantime the Quiroga cabinet was kept in a continual state of agitation, trying in vain to settle the strikes. Through June and the first half of July all the workers in the building trades of Madrid and the surrounding provinces were on strike for higher wages and shorter hours, a united movement with the support of both the *U.G.T.* and the *C.N.T.* For weeks they steadfastly refused government arbitration—a triumph of Syndicalist policy. When the *U.G.T.* finally decided to conduct a secret ballot on whether they should begin negotiations for a settlement through the government agencies, the *C.N.T.* denounced this as vile knuckling to the bourgeois state. While the controversy was dragging on, the streets of the capital were filled with able-bodied men forced to beg for a morsel because the unions had no money for relief. When the *U.G.T.* actually submitted to government arbitration the leaders of the *C.N.T.* prepared to send their men into action against the "scabs," as they had in Malaga. Only the firing of fascist guns in the Montaña barracks on the morning of July 18 welded these two sections of the proletariat together.

Anarchist grievances harassed the government in other spheres. The anarchists were in no wise satisfied with the amnesty for political prisoners which the cabinet had proclaimed as soon as it came into office. They filled the columns of their newspapers with stories about innocent victims who had falsely been accused of burning churches and autobuses and who were not included in any of the decrees of liberation. What about the starving workers who had stolen during the economic crisis and were not reckoned among the political offenders? Was it not monstrous that foreign anarchists should still languish in the prisons of the Spanish Republic at a time when all groups of the People's Front were zealous in their demonstrations in behalf of Germany's Thälmann or Brazil's Luis Carlos Prestes? The anarchists remained the problem children of the Republic, and in spite of the increase in the number of so-called "reasonable anarchists" since the Franco rebellion their political actions still border on delinquency.

Prieto's Pyrrhic Victory

While the strikes and the propaganda of the Anarcho-Syndicalists raged through the country the Socialist Party continued to provide the main topic of political discussion in the first summer days of 1936. Toward the end of June the controversy between the rivals entered a rather pedantic constitutional phase when each side accused the other of departing from the rules and regulations of the Socialist Party. Caballero once again demanded an immediate general congress of the whole party; the Prietist Executive Committee deemed the moment inopportune. Caballero, using the Madrid section of the party as a starting-point, initiated agitation through the country for a referendum on the meeting-date of the party congress, expecting a popular censure of the Executive Committee. The Prietists countered with articles from the party constitution to the effect that only the Executive Committee had the right to call for a referendum.

Debate was still swirling about this issue when elections were held for vacant seats on the Executive Committee, a contest which came to be regarded as a test of strength for the opposing factions, an indirect declaration of policy on the problem of collaboration. Unfortunately, instead of clarifying the air the election brought new occasion for mutual vilification.

While the standing Executive Committee pointedly insisted that this was to be a ballot only for vacant seats, the followers of Caballero with equal insistence sent in complete lists for a wholly new committee. Thereupon the Prietists invalidated the Left Socialist votes which had not complied with their orders. The results published in *El Socialista* gave González Peña, the Socialist leader of the Asturias and Prieto's candidate, 11,000 votes, to a mere 1,500 for Caballero. When it was revealed that a total of only 23,000 votes (including invalidated ballots) had been cast in the whole election, the figures became the subject of grave consideration. Though Caballero may have had the masses behind him in the bullring meetings, his audiences did not possess party books, did not pay dues, and could not officially record their desires in local Socialist units. It was soon reported that even old members, if they had failed to pay dues, had been deprived of their votes. Prieto's control over the party bureaucracy had proved crucial. The Left Socialists, upon hearing the returns, rent the air with their cries of indignation. What right had the officials of the Socialist bureaucracy to throw out the votes of those who had not paid their membership dues? Was this a bar to participation in the balloting of a proletarian party at a time when thousands were on strike and workers needed every penny to keep their wives and children from starving? Was this handful of voters to determine the policy of the Socialist Party, upon whom the whole future of the government depended? The nonsocialist press, more than other organs, disclosed the true meaning of the elections. Liberal bourgeois and reactionary newspapers, *El Sol* and *A.B.C.*, joined in celebrating the "Centrist" victory. The danger from revolutionary Caballero had passed.

In the corridors of the Cortes deputies from all parties flocked about Prieto—the next prime minister, perhaps—extending their congratulations. Even Socialist deputies, who had previously been divided about equally between the two rival leaders, now tendered new testimonials of loyalty to the victor. Only *Claridad* and *Mundo Obrero* denounced the legalist maneuver which had falsified the will of the people. News of an army uprising in Morocco broke upon the country before this party conflict was resolved. For a number of months Largo Caballero and Indalecio Prieto buried the hatchet—where it could be found again—and joined in defense of the Republic.[2]

NOTES

1. Various official and unofficial agencies, both loyalist and rebel, have drawn up flagrantly contradictory statistics on the popular vote for the Cortes elections of 1936. The figures which have been presented vary because: (1) the 130,000 traditionalist, though pro-Republic, Basque Nationalists are claimed by both the Left and the Right; (2) there was a second balloting on March 1 which made for confusion in estimating popular totals; (3) in some districts the Right and the Center presented joint lists of candidates, while in other districts the Center and the Left were thus allied; (4) there were a number of Independents who could be aligned *ad lib.;* and (5) the elections of Cuenca and Granada, annulled by the Cortes, were held again on May 3, 1936, so that one could accept or refuse the results of the new balloting.

    Attempts to use the election results as decisive factors in determining the "morality" of the rebellion seem futile since: (1) the election machinery was in most cases controlled by Rightists; (2) hundreds of thousands of Anarcho-Syndicalists failed to vote; (3) tens of thousands of political prisoners in jail since October, 1934, could not vote; and (4) those who voted Right or Center in February, 1936, did not thereby sanction the rebellion.

2. This chapter is based upon notes taken by the author during interviews with leaders both of the People's Front and of the Rightist parties.

Chapter IX

THE FASCIST COUNTERATTACK

Almost immediately after Prime Minister Quiroga delivered his first forceful discourses in the Cortes on May 19, 1936, doubts were cast on the possible longevity of his cabinet. There was an air of transience and frustration about all its movements. Deputies of the Right, to show their ill feeling toward the Republic and to obstruct proceedings, refused to participate in the work of the parliamentary commissions. Spasmodically an exchange of insults between the Right and the Left enlivened the sessions, and every few weeks the Cortes staged dramatic debates on the state of the nation during which Gil Robles and Calvo Sotelo poured forth their homemade statistics on the churches which had been destroyed, on general strikes declared, and on political assassinations which remained mysterious. The figures were intended to focus the attention of the people on anarchy in the land. Indeed, nothing was more fitting than that the Catholic demagogue and the monarchist should present the details of incidents which their own agents were provoking.

During the parliamentary debates international news services with a fine show of sympathy flashed the record of rape and arson over their wires, outdoing the Spanish reactionaries in stressing gruesome details. Before France voted a People's Front victory in the May elections of 1936 *Agence Havas* featured Spanish horrors, a bloody warning to the middle-class Frenchman that he had better turn to the Right or he too would be terrorized by the Marxists. Official Germany and Italy with perfected instruments of persuasion were arousing sentiment among their peoples against the Red Spanish destroyers of civilization. Spain's incendiaries even figured in the first blasts of the anti-Roosevelt campaign in 1936 as an example of the radical road to ruin.

At home Prime Minister Quiroga made a strenuous endeavor to cope with the reaction and its provocators. The Agrarian Reform Law revoked by the clerical-fascists in the 1935 *Contra-*

reforma agraria was passed for a second time; the new Minister of Agriculture, Ruiz Funes, executed it with a dispatch unknown under the first republican coalition. Two hundred thousand peasants were settled on the land in the Toledo district, in the province of Salamanca, and in Andalucía. Novel experiments were conducted in agricultural communes such as Malpica and Móstoles. Revival of the program of secular education under Barnés, who in the Cortes once more attacked the "base system of the Jesuits," infuriated the Rightists. Laws against outspoken fascist judges stimulated their spokesmen to defend the so-called independence of the judiciary. A limited number of ambassadorial transfers in the spirit of the People's Front brought mournful reflections on Spain's waning glory abroad.

Landowners and Industrialists

But spirited anti-fascists could not be satiated with halfway measures. The congress of secular schoolteachers which met in Madrid's Socialist trade-union hall and swiftly aligned itself with Caballero, had little praise for the Left Republican ministers who, its resolution claimed, still permitted reactionary inspectors to lord over the educational system. The assembled schoolteachers, whose faces reflected years of struggle with local *caciques* and priests, demanded higher wages, better equipped buildings, and training schools freed from fascist professors. Most of the pleas remained unheeded because of the government's financial embarrassment, though the state did attempt to stifle fascism in the universities. The Madrid Law School was closed down because young fascists were emphasizing their political allegiance in the classroom with pistol shots. The university students, who were almost invariably of the upper middle class, had in 1931 constituted the vanguard of republicanism. Now, to the distraction of the authorities, they responded to their established class sympathies and became an important recruiting field for the Spanish Phalanx. It was *à la mode* for upper middle-class intellectuals to admire fascist valor. When a foreign visitor called the attention of an official in the Ministry of Education to the blatant fascist complexion of the academic teaching body and asked why they had not been dismissed, the reply was characteristic of the whole regime: "You ask me: why? Indeed, I ask you: why? This is a democratic republic."[1]

During the spring the counterattack of the landowners and the industrialists was assuming new forms. In small country towns secret societies of employers sprang into being. Their members vowed never to submit to the demands of the laborers. A violation of this sacred oath was threatened with death. In one of the richest agricultural districts Almedralejo, the landowners refused to sow, and since in impoverished Spain there was no provision for unemployment relief, starvation spread within a few days throughout the area. In the cities, employers sabotaged every effort of government intervention during strikes. Official boards of arbitration decided upon a plan of conciliation; the employers refused it; fines fixed by law were imposed as a measure of coercion; the employers appealed to the ministry for redress; though denied a remedy they remained adamant. To evade administrative action, suits were then lodged with the ordinary tribunals; strikes were intentionally prolonged, for employers could always count on the ravages of hunger to force workers into withdrawing their demands. When toward the end of June the government, piqued into activity by the dilatory maneuvers of manufacturers, ventured to make an example of the contumacious owners of elevator repair shops in Madrid imposing upon them a fine of 400,000 pesetas, the Republic was confronted by a solidified employer class organized for concerted action. Since the fine was not paid, the most defiant shop owners were imprisoned. Thereupon the entrepreneurs of the building trades, out of sympathy for members of their class, stalked out of the conference which was negotiating a strike settlement for construction workers. Late in June the determined hostility of employers, coupled with the intransigence of the Anarcho-Syndicalists, left 150,000 strikers on the streets of the capital.

For skilled work in cities eight pesetas a day (the peseta was worth about fifteen cents) was considered a high wage; agricultural workers were known to earn less than two pesetas a day. Moreover, the incidence of taxation was such that the brunt of the national burden fell upon the mass of the people through indirect levies, while the Conde de Romanones, the richest man in Madrid, was relatively untouched. Flores de Lemus who early in July was perfunctorily drawing up new tax laws for the Ministry of Finance, still felt that the lottery was the ideal form of taxation. He praised even its religious character, because of the element of hope which it introduced into the lives of the poor worker and the wretched peasant. And the lottery remained one of the principal sources of income for the government at a time when tax evasion safeguarded the wealth of the upper classes. Spain's Treasury was too near bankruptcy, one was informed in the summer of 1936, to afford relief for the unemployed. Estimates of the unemployed varied from the official notion of a few hundred thousand to the Communist Party's more plausible figure of 1,000,000. And yet a renovation of the tax system was one of the daring feats to be postponed to some future date.

In the meantime reactionaries with and without titles who could lay hold of fluid assets were exporting them from the country. Nobles stripped their palaces of Spain's artistic patrimony and sold their paintings to English connoisseurs in order to assure themselves a well-furnished haven of refuge. When applied to modern Spain the Marxist dictum, "The worker has no fatherland," needs emendation. The draining of pesetas from Spain was leading to the disruption of the country's economy. Government decrees which ordained that no individual might export more than 5,000 pesetas, and then only by special permit, were inefficacious. Europe was flooded with Spanish currency. In French border towns like St. Jean de Luz pesetas which had been smuggled across could be bought at 30 to 50 per cent below the quoted price. Foreign capitalists frantically tried to salvage their Spanish investments before the day of doom about which they were reading. Monks who had to submit to unceremonious examinations in customs offices revealed hauls of thousands of pesetas beneath their cowls.

The Spanish Phalanx

How was the government to defend itself? Its hope had been, and Prieto's too, that when peace was reestablished in employer-worker relations the bourgeois would be reassured, foreigners would dispel their fears, and Spain's vast industrial potentialities would be exploited for the greater happiness of all Spaniards. But this was a futile hope. Unemployment insurance, pensions for the aged, paid vacations, the forty-hour week, the reforms which the French working class had won through their peaceful sit-down strikes of July, were fantastic dreams for chaotic Spain. Here there were long-drawn-out strikes, and with the strikes economic uneasiness, which engendered lockouts, a vicious circle from which there seemed no escape, because the dominant classes were preparing for war—class war.

Those who knew Madrid fascists felt that by April their sponsors had completely recovered from the shock of the People's Front victory. Plans for a military uprising were laid early; they were in part common knowledge, though few suspected the extent to which international fascism was the tutor of the movement. Fascist prestige on the continent had been greatly enhanced by Mussolini's conquest of Ethiopia and by the implied humiliation of Britain and France. The daring of the Italian enterprise in contempt of the League of Nations and its sanctions spurred on reactionaries of all countries to press for audacious action. In May Spanish fascists celebrated Victor Emmanuel's proclamation as Emperor of Ethiopia with dinner parties; upon the report of Italian triumphs the Spanish Rightists passionately described the natural heroic virtues of the Latin race to which both nations belonged. Germans were ordinarily too much identified with secular culture to be favorites of reactionary Spaniards, and the human specimens who came to Spain to direct industrial enterprises were not popular. Hitler, nevertheless, found his way regularly onto the rotogravure front page of *A.B.C.*, alternating with pictures of the glories which he was bestowing upon the New Germany.

When the People's Front made it apparent that this time they were determined to break the economic backbone of old Spain, the competing Rightist parties abandoned their squabbles. Calvo Sotelo, the monarchist leader, frankly admitted a few weeks before his assassination that 98 per cent of the Rightists were now fascist. When questioned about the type of government he ideally envisaged for Spain, he described something in between the Portuguese and the Italian models. He talked of respect for the Catholic tradition, protection of property, the end of anarchy, and the docility of the proletariat whenever a strong ruler revealed himself. Sotelo was undoubtedly one of the few capable nonmilitary administrators on the Right, and he was cut out for a vital role after the fascist victory. His assassination on July 13 left the Rightists no other prominent politicians but Gil Robles of the Popular Action and young José Primo de Rivera, the head of the Spanish Phalanx. The son of the former dictator was soon to meet his end in a republican prison. Thus Gil Robles was left alone—a rather flabby figure adequate for parliamentary obstruction, useful at most as a liaison agent during a deadly struggle. Juan March, capitalist friend of the Jesuits and former smuggler and grafter, was perhaps the most conspicuous nonmilitary conspirator, and at first he held the money bags for the rebels. When the movement passed far beyond the sphere of even his millions, March became Franco's ambassador extraordinary fluttering about Europe on secret missions. Thus an uprising which had begun as the common enterprise of ranking clerics, financiers, monarchists, Catholic demagogues, and official fascists, utilizing the military as a divine scourge, fell completely into the hands of a clique of army generals and their mentors from abroad. The monster came to rule those who fashioned it.

For months before the rebellion a spirit of anarchy had been generated through the land, a temper of uneasiness which would make the indifferent middle sector of the population welcome a man on horseback who would establish order. Mystical anarcho-syndicalists who threw bombs and perpetrated petty acts of terror fostered this mood gratuitously. When the disorders proved inadequate the fascists could readily buy degenerate provocators in a hungry Spain. Sections of the slum proletariat (*Lumpenproletariat*) were allowed to ease their way into the syndicalist federation of labor. Dues in the *C.N.T.* were lower than in the *U.G.T*; anarcho-syndicalist discipline was rather slipshod, on principle; and fascists who had crept into the organization were now able to counsel acts of violence under the guise of revolutionary ardor.

Since May, 1936, facts about abortive fascist conspiracies were sometimes publicized, but more often they were allowed to remain police secrets. The record of assassination was kept hidden. On May 2 a few soldiers, a few peasants, and a lawyer, Pardo Reina, were arrested as agents of a plot. Who was behind them? A few days later a mutiny of the troops had to be put down in Alcalá de Henares. Since the government was allowed so many foretastes of the great rebellion, why then did it not seek out the enemy in its own camp? The Spanish Phalanx, though its ranks had swelled since the February elections, was no mass party in the sense that Hitler's Nazis were before the seizure of power.   The Falangists were largely troops of paid gangsters and students drunk with the romanticism of fascist phraseology. If there was to be a *coup d'état*, and divinators were not needed to interpret the portents, the primary agents of revolt would be the old arbiters of Spanish politics, the army, or rather both armies: the official military establishment destined for foreign wars and the Civil Guard, peacetime protector of the state.   Had the government at any time felt itself strong enough to dominate these praetorian forces, the military-fascist uprising would have been postponed, at least until it was confronted by a fully consolidated People's Front.

The Civil Guard

The Guards of Assault, the semimilitary corps which the Republican government had created for its own defense, were weak compared to the Civil Guard.   This body had been conspicuous in the repression of the Asturian uprising of 1934.   The election of the People's Front was a victory of the masses; thus on the morrow of the Left's electoral triumph the Civil Guards awaited serious reprisals.   They were astounded when these were in nowise so severe as might have been expected.   Many a commander of the Guard who, like Doval, had indulged in extreme barbarity in the Asturias, was allowed to leave the mainland on a mission of police investigation.   The government transferred some officers, demoted others, and dismissed the most notorious of its enemies, but retained as a body 35,000 men whom it knew to be permeated with fascist sympathies.   Even if the Civil Guard had desired to be loyal to the republican government the peasants would not have accepted the conversion, for among them hatred strikes deep roots.   Suspicion would not die out. Time and again the proletarian parties threatened to demand the dissolution of the whole corps.   The government wavered, and no one ventured to disrupt the People's Front over this issue.

There were, however, moments when it seemed that the proletarian parties could no longer endanger their own existence by the retention of the Guard.   On May 29 an incident occurred in Yeste, a town in the province of Albacete, which brought the ominous name Casas Viejas back to everyone's lips.   A village tragedy had sealed Azaña's doom in 1933. Was the same to be Quiroga's fate? As usual a week passed before the details of this new clash between the Civil Guards and the peasants crept through the stringent press censorship. On the evening of June 5 the government agreed to submit to an interpellation in the Cortes; the Rightists filled their benches to watch the People's Front disintegrate, and ambassadors crowded into their special gallery. The Socialist deputy Prat presented his version of the events at Yeste: When the villagers attempted to seize a piece of private property which had once been part of the village commons, the Civil Guards drove forth the intruders and arrested the ringleaders. Rumor spread that the captive peasants were being tortured in the local prison. The villagers rushed out to free their comrades, and during a hand-to-hand combat one guard was killed. Thereupon the infuriated patrol massacred 17 peasants. Eyewitnesses told of a peasant woman who was ordered to lie down and was then shot in cold blood. Three laborers were found dead in sewers. . . . The Communist deputy Mitje, in somewhat more violent tones, blamed the local *caciques* for the Yeste tragedy. Then the Minister of the Interior arose to promise a full investigation and prompt punishment. The People's Front was saved, for no party wanted to bear responsibility for the downfall of the government.

The Civil Guards were cleansed, but allowed to continue their reign. When the rebellion of July 18 broke out observers were at first astonished to find the Guards fighting the fascist army alongside of the popular militia. The allegiance of the Guards seemed proof of the immediate superiority of the government forces and bolstered the Republic's faith in a quick victory. But whatever trust was then placed in the Civil Guards turned out to be premature. At crucial moments many of them betrayed the government and joined Franco's forces. A division of sentiment within this military police was all that Left-Republican manipulation of officers and privates could accomplish.

Sulking Generals

The government's method of one day cajoling and the next day intimidating into submission the regular army corps was an even more fatal error. The military could not be seduced with pensions. They really believed in their task as the liberators

of Spain from the "Marxist rabble" whom they despised.
There were no possibilities of compromise with men imagining
themselves the counterparts of those Prussian officers who had
trained them in the Spanish Foreign Legion. With the rebirth
of the military ideal in Western Europe, the Continent seemed to
be reverting to a pattern of honor and nobility, of which the
Spanish officer corps had fancied themselves the guardians
throughout the democratic period. Spain had a long tradition
of military dictatorship to hark back to. In the eyes of the
government, the army was a body difficult to integrate into the
Republican scheme; to the generals, the army was an *alternative*
to the government.

"Why have eight regiments? One is enough!" was Araquistáin's comment during a discussion of the menace of a military
uprising. Spain had no foreign enemies; the establishment in
Morocco was a profitless burden. Azaña's outlook was somewhat
different: with the example of England and France before him
he would educate the generals to a conception of their duty as
the custodians of national defense. Yet on more than one
occasion they proved themselves refractory; hence General
Franco, though he had already been head of the War College at
Saragossa, was transferred to the Canary Islands to reflect on
his misdemeanors. Goded was sent to the Balearic Islands.
Under sunny skies they were allowed to hibernate and to hatch
plans for an uprising. "Turismo," as it was jocularly called—
the transfer of dangerous military elements from strategic positions to apparently less significant posts off the peninsula—was a
poor technique for disciplining soldiers.

While the rebel plot was being brewed Prime Minister Quiroga,
who was also Minister of War, sought a hundred officers whom he
could trust fully in order to station them at points of vantage
throughout the country. After combing the entire army he
discovered only sixty odd men, evidence of the political inflexi-
bility of the corps. Neither were the rank and file of soldiers
much more reliable. Army officers loyal to the Republic, driven
almost to distraction by the insoluble problem before them,
remarked upon the peculiar transformation which a simple
peasant's son underwent once he was put into a uniform. A
distinction, however, must be made between soldiers isolated in
the barracks of provincial towns and alienated from their peasant

surroundings and detachments stationed in large cities like Madrid and Barcelona, where the soldier, during frequent contacts with the mass of the people in meeting halls and amusement places, came to understand popular aspirations. In the metropolitan areas the rebel generals who proclaimed the uprising a defense of the "true republic" and a struggle against Marxism found that their men were no dupes. Soldiers turned their guns against the fascist officers and allied themselves with the people.

In May and June—as a counterweight to the army, the Civil Guards, and the fascist bands—the proletarian parties urged the creation of a popular militia. This body might have finally destroyed the prestige of the army, and perhaps the fear of its eventual creation spurred the generals on to action, though as long as the bourgeois Republicans were in power such anxiety was groundless. Even though he usually addressed himself only to the Left, Quiroga, like Janus, could look both ways. With Largo Caballero eulogizing the proletarian dictatorship and the anarcho-syndicalists making forays into the realm of libertarian communism the government refused to arm the people. Even after the rebellion had begun, Azaña allowed a number of days to elapse before he actually distributed guns. Before July 18 it was considered a hazardous concession when the government tolerated the amateurish drilling of the Left Socialist and Communist militia. After union meetings, there were collections of money for the purchase of arms, and workers whose pay was hardly enough to feed them contributed their pittance. Before the actual outbreak young militiamen stayed awake nights, prepared for a call at any moment. Here was the nucleus of that People's Army which saved a government that had not dared to save itself.

Republican Turncoats

The ideological frills which accompanied the military uprising were less ornate than if this had been a fascist movement in the German manner. A simple military campaign needs arms and a quartermaster, perhaps a priest for benediction, but its scribes are not overesteemed. There were, however, enough professors, intellectuals, and nondescript politicians who, without immediate compensation, were willing to herald the coming of the man whose name was not mentioned. Republican turncoats were among the loudest trumpeters. On June 26, Miguel Maura, one of the founding fathers, envisaged his ideal national government in just these words: "It will be an organ of neutralized passions and of functional dynamism." In private conversation Miguel de Unamuno, patriarch of the Republic, expressed his contempt for the People's Front with unprintable ejaculations. "Who knows what fascism may bring?" he hopefully mused. Abandoning his world-renowned reflections on death he turned to writing signed editorials for *Ahora*, the conservative Madrid newspaper with the largest circulation. In his contribution of June 5, he devoted himself to ridiculing the first article of the Republican Constitution, which exalted the ideal of the productive worker. "Labor! Labor! What isn't labor? Has the concept of labor ever been as fertile as love and death? Has it ever inspired a poem like Leopardi's *Amore e Morte?* If this notion keeps gaining ground we shall soon have beggars as 'workers of mendicity,' the shock troops as 'workers of repression,' and the unemployed as 'workers of consumption.'"

On July 18 Unamuno hailed the coming of General Franco, and from his Rector's chair in the University of Salamanca he wrote Latin epistles to university presidents throughout the world denouncing the Republican government. A few months later he died an embittered man, having seen German troops goose-step through the streets of his beloved Salamanca. . . . Salvador de Madariaga's fate was less dramatic. His essays in *Ahora*, entitled *Revolution and Capitalism*, struck a high point on June 21 when he announced: "I absolutely refuse to grow sentimental over the poor workers." Though it was at one time rumored that England was building him up as an arbiter of the present Spanish conflict, the academician and diplomat selected a less burdensome task by lecturing in American universities and before American women's clubs. Other personalities of Spain's old intellectual élite who had never felt the material want of their people glibly attacked the Republic. Then, at the apparition of the military boot, they took fright and mumbled, "A plague on both your houses," though, unlike Mercutio, they did not always die.

During the night of July 11, José Castillo, a favorite officer among the Republican shock troops was killed by fascists assassins. The next day at dawn a police car filled with men in shock troop uniforms[2] drew up to Calvo Sotelo's Madrid apartment and ordered him to the police station for questioning. By afternoon his body, riddled with bullets, was found in the cemetery of Almudena. Sotelo's death provided the rebellion with a signal; forces which had been held in check for an autumn uprising were now unleashed.

NOTES

1. This chapter is based upon notes taken by the author during interviews with leaders both of the People's Front and of the Rightist parties.
2. Their identity has not been conclusively established.

Epilogue

During the early days of the rebellion all Spain was a no man's land. How could enemies identify each other when they met in an isolated village in the Guadarrama mountains? All seemed to reiterate similar phrases. And yet life or death depended upon the moment of recognition. By now Spain has been divided into two parts, and trenches have been dug along a winding front.

The Emergence of Republican Discipline

The romantic period during which a People's Militia of old men with hunting guns, boys with sticks, and girls in overalls marched to the firing line, could not last for many months, glorious as the early days of mass enthusiasm were. Even government ministers, in defiance of laws on the division of labor, felt it their duty to present themselves for action a few hours each day lest they be considered bureaucratic cowards. More than a year passed before the defenders of the Republic were molded into a regular army force. Loyal military officers were none too numerous, and while the masses cherished the few who remained by their side through the first days of bewilderment, the people had to be vigilant and guard against treachery in their own general staff. Some loyal officers were at best mediocre; in crucial positions it was impossible to draw a line between sloth, defeatism, and treason. The rising peasants, workers, and middle-class city dwellers had to entrust the fate of the Republic to military men many of whom lacked faith. The armaments of the government were negligible. Spaniards had never learned to fight in a World War; peasants who had worked the soil with primitive instruments could not easily learn to use modern mechanical equipment. Military observers of the great industrial nations of the world made sport of the poor marksmanship and the lack of technical skill. Republican army officers were not free from professional skepticism when they had to lead their shabby, ill-fed, poorly armed civilians against the Moorish

184

cavalry, the hardened Foreign Legion, and the battalions from fascist Germany and Italy.

In bureaucratic Madrid idealist ambivalence remained enthroned for many months. On the pronouncement of the rebellion Martínez Barrio, a Right Republican, was summoned to head the cabinet; upon protest from the proletarian parties he was superseded by Giralt, an honest Left Republican. Only when Largo Caballero became premier of a coalition government including all parties of the People's Front—Communists as well as Anarchists—did the Popular Militia grow more confident of its political leadership. Caballero, however, grew dictatorial without justifying his presumption by a display of organizational talents. Members of his own cabinet—Socialist, Communist, and Anarchist representatives, living proof of the unity of the proletariat—were kept in ignorance of military and civil policy. The premier chose his own generals, refused the advice of other cabinet members, and seemed determined to win the war personally. When behind the closed doors of cabinet meetings the Communists ventured to censure the actions of a loyalist general, Caballero interpreted the criticism as a personal affront, an expression of disloyalty to his government. The Communists chafed, but continued to tolerate the antics of the Spanish Lenin whom they themselves had erected.

When months before the siege of Madrid the Communists pleaded for the fortification of the city they were decried as alarmists. On November 9 the capital was saved only by Russian arms, the International Anti-Fascist Brigade, the cool competence of General Miaja, who assumed responsibility after the ministers had fled to Valencia, and the passion which transfigured the populace. A government which had waited until the trenches in the University City had to be dug by civilians under fire could not endure. In May, 1937, the Communists joined with energetic leaders like Indalecio Prieto to oust Caballero and his group. The fallen premier still had control over the Socialist trade-union executive, and he could play upon the anticommunism of some syndicalist workers. But the countermovement which he engineered, though troublesome, was ineffectual. With Negrín, a mild Socialist, as premier and Prieto as Minister of National Defense, the Madrid front was reorganized and "unity of command" became a reality—too late, however, to save Bilbao and the Asturias. Today there are in fact indications that Republican Spain's newly consolidated industries will produce enough war materials to free it from absolute dependence upon Russian imports. The victory of Teruel bears testimony.

During the first days of the people's triumph over the fascists in Catalonia heroism and vandalism were intermingled. In some sections of Barcelona gangsters parading as anarchists held sway; the rebellion brought the scum of a Mediterranean port to the surface. Once victory at home was assured the Popular Militia of the *Generalitat* did not surge forward to the defense of Madrid. Troops marching back and forth from the Aragón front disgusted observers with their political sectarianism and separatism. "We have made our revolution, let the Madrid people make theirs," was the dominant sentiment. Republicans and anarchists jockeyed for positions. The P.O.U.M. (Workers' Party of Marxist Unity) established itself as an agglomeration of dissident communist elements among which Trotsky's emissaries found a hunting ground. Parading violent revolutionary slogans they spurred the anarchists on to seek measures out of harmony with the broad anti-fascist policy of the People's Front. In such loose organizations fascist sympathizers and spies had an easy job. A revolt of Trotskyists and Anarchists in May, 1937, had to be suppressed by forces from Madrid. Only since General Franco's advance toward Catalonia has the new Negrín cabinet been able to revitalize the Republican troops of the *Generalitat.*

Captains of the Rebellion

In rebel Spain the military leaders have proceeded with a minimum of internecine quarrels. Except for minor distractions —Franco's execution of Manuel Hedilla, a chieftain of the Fascist Party, and the shooting of troops who complained about food being snatched from their mouths to be eaten by the Italian allies—the military machine ruthlessly strives to fulfill the plans laid out by German and Italian staff officers. A captured city, whatever the weapon, means victory; the inhabitants are enemies until they prove the contrary.

Oddly enough, in the 1920's most of the leaders of the present rebellion belonged to a republican masonic lodge known as the

Fraternal Military Union, a clique hostile to the monarchy.[1] They participated in the overthrow of Alfonso XIII; their abandonment of the King in the spring of 1931 alleviated the labor pains of the Republic. General Queipo de Llano and Commandant Franco, brother of the rebel chief, engineered a conspiracy of artillery men and aviators who threatened to blow up the royal palace unless Alfonso surrendered. General Goded was chosen to rouse the army in Madrid if the King resisted; General Sanjurjo, head of the Civil Guard, intimated that he stood by the people; General Mola, the prefect of police in the capital, refused to suppress demonstrations against Alfonso. When five years later the same men revolted to reestablish the dignity of the warrior, internal rivalries among them might have been disastrous to their cause had not death drawn lots for them. After Sanjurjo—who was to have led the rebellion—was killed in an airplane flying from Portugal; after Goded, the "general of the señoritas," was executed at Barcelona following a judgment by the People's Tribunal; after General Fanjul suffered a similar fate at Madrid; and after General Mola crashed in another airplane accident, a long process of elimination came to an end from which Francisco Franco emerged as the undisputed master, *El Caudillo.* Queipo de Llano, one of the few surviving leaders, was granted monopoly over the radio station in Seville, and he seemed content with his daily broadcasts.

A military directorate, centralized about General Franco, has been established at Salamanca; terror has replaced forms of civil life: "One Fatherland, one State, one Chief!" There may be a restoration of the Bourbons, or the army men may organize their own state, depending upon political and diplomatic exigencies. The official Fascist Party, the Spanish Phalanx, and the monarchist Carlists are too insignificant to influence seriously the actions of the central *junta* of officers whose word is now law.

Of all the generals Francisco Franco was the one least tainted by masonic affiliations. In rebel Spain the church has again been placed upon its sacred throne. A religious revival by order of Franco has been its reward for making arsenals of holy places and for opening its coffers to finance a crusade against the Marxist-Judaic-Masonic heresy. But since Catholicism has not in the past sufficed as the protective ideology of reactionary Spain, it is being mixed with the backwash of fascist metaphysics

from Germany and Italy. Rationalism is open to daily attack
in the accustomed manner:

Opposed to the intellectuals who grow sterilely ecstatic before
problems, Spain needs mystics to lead the genius of our destiny, that
amor fati which the ancient Romans and later Sorel and Nietzsche
preached, that *amor fati* of deeds, of the grand realities of each country,
which impelled Mussolini into action, to create fascism. Spain needs
mystics who shall proclaim as the supreme dignity of man, of Spanish
man, not the felicity of comfort or of material progress, but the ad-
venturesome life, the creative danger, the tragic feeling of existence,
men for whom the words sorrow and war have an affirmative, noble
meaning.[2]

Franco's Spain thus panders to the "great irrationals" of
fascism, and there is much in Spanish tradition upon which it
may draw. The mystics of the church, the obscurantists and
the lay pseudomystics of reactionary journalism denounce
science and idealize ritual purification through blood. The
scribes who crawl before the warriors extol the grandeur of wanton
vigor, the beauties of brutality, and the religious virtue of suffering. Moorish luxury for the lords of society and privation for
their subjects is a normal consequence of murky idealism. To
bolster vague conceptions the creators of the rebel ideology have
dipped into racial theory, though their own use of the Moorish
mercenaries makes it embarrassing to impute the spread of
communism to the infusion of semitic blood into the original
Iberian, Phoenician, Greek, Roman, and Visigothic strains of
the inhabitants of the peninsula. The Spanish Republic is being
identified with Judaism in an attempt to strike an atavistic,
though effective note. Reports from fascist Spain do not, however, indicate that the men and women in rebel territory have
been moved by a resurrection of the weird images of the Inquisi-
tor's ceremonial.

The Republic has preserved the legal forms of democracy with
care, though the world steadfastly refused to be impressed by
the fact that the Cortes has held its annual October meeting in
accordance with the constitution of 1931. The Republic still
represents the belief in the power of reason to order life and a
desire to improve the physical and spiritual well-being of the
entire people. If this be communism, then let reactionaries
make the most of it. To millions of Spaniards the Republic

means life.   To them Franco's reign is symbolized by the armless, eyeless General Millán Astray shouting in his madness: "Down with Intelligence!   Long Live Death!"[3]

NOTES

1. Jérôme and Jean Tharaud, *Cruelle Espagne*, pp. 34–35, Paris, 1937.
2. *Faro de Vigo*, Dec. 11, 1936, p. 8.
3. Ramón Sender, *Counter-Attack in Spain*, p. 137, Boston, 1937.

INDEX